OXFORD LATIN READER

TEACHER'S BOOK

MAURICE BALME & JAMES MORWOOD
OXFORD UNIVERSITY PRESS

OXFORD
UNIVERSITY PRESS

Great Clarendon Street, Oxford OX2 6DP

Oxford University Press is a department of the University of Oxford.
It furthers the University's objective of excellence in research,
scholarship, and education by publishing worldwide in

Oxford   New York

Auckland   Cape Town   Dar es Salaam   Hong Kong   Karachi
Kuala Lumpur   Madrid   Melbourne   Mexico City   Nairobi
New Delhi   Shanghai   Taipei   Toronto

With offices in

Argentina   Austria   Brazil   Chile   Czech Republic   France   Greece
Guatemala   Hungary   Italy   Japan   Poland   Portugal   Singapore
South Korea   Switzerland   Thailand   Turkey   Ukraine   Vietnam

Oxford is a registered trade mark of Oxford University Press
in the UK and in certain other countries

© Oxford University Press 1997

British Library Cataloguing in Publication Data

Data available

ISBN-13: 978-0-19-912233-2

20 19 18 17 16 15 14 13

Printed in Great Britain by Bell & Bain, Glasgow

Acknowledgements

The publisher and authors are most grateful to the following for granting permission to include translations from the Oxford World's Classics series: Carolyn Hammond (extracts from Caesar: The Gallic War), Guy Lee (extracts from poems of Catullus) and Mrs Melville on behalf of A.D. Melville (extracts from Ovid: The Love Poems; Ovid: Metamorphoses, and Ovid: Sorrows of an Exile).

Contents

Introduction

This Reader forms the fourth part of the Oxford Latin Course. The first three parts cover most basic grammar and syntax and introduce a fair amount of unadapted Latin in Part III, including extracts from Horace's poetry. The narrative centres around the life of Horace, covering the period of the late Republic and the Augustan age, so that some of the historical and cultural background to our authors will already be familiar to students who have used the course.

The Reader is introduced by a brief historical sketch of the late Republic from the Gracchi to the death of Sulla; some knowledge of these events is necessary to understand the careers of Cicero and Caesar. Events following the death of Sulla are described in the commentary linking the extracts from Cicero, which are arranged in biographical sequence. We do not provide a general introduction to the the lives of the last three authors; Part III of the course gives a fairly full account of the Augustan revolution and we did not wish to repeat all this. Teachers who have not used the earlier parts of the course may feel the need to fill this gap briefly.

Nor do we provide the traditional essay on the style of the authors, since we believe that the study of form apart from content is unhelpful and will only encourage students to regurgitate conventional opinion. But we do from time to time draw attention to stylistic features of passages as they occur in the text being read, and suggest in the Teacher's Book questions that might be asked. If students are encouraged to see for themselves from the study of particular passages what the author is trying to do and how he achieves it, they will gain a far more real understanding and appreciation of the author's 'style'. In the case of Catullus, we do give questions of a critical nature after most poems, including some comparisons of translations, for we feel that such detailed critical questions are appropriate in the handling of short lyric poems.

In Parts I to III, we glossed all unknown words in the margin of the text. In the Reader we gloss only difficult words or usages; students must at this stage learn to use the vocabulary as a dictionary. We give two appendices in the Reader. The first is a select vocabulary of common words that have occurred in the authors read and that were not learnt in the chapter vocabularies of Parts I to III. At this stage the acquisition of a wide vocabulary is vital to achieving fluent reading. The second appendix gives a brief account of the metres used by Catullus, Virgil and Ovid. In Part III this was confined to the Teacher's Book, but we thought that in this Reader students should be able to study metrics for themselves.

We have decided not to insert macra over the long vowels in the main text on the grounds that students will have learnt correct pronunciation in Parts I to III of the course and must now do without this prop. But we have put in macra in both the select and general vocabularies in which new words occur. Teachers should make sure that students' pronunciation is correct, paying particular attention to the final **-a** of 1st declension nominative and ablative and the final **-is** of 3rd declension nouns (the accusative plural form in **-is**, regularly used by Caesar and Virgil, has long **i**).

In the Teacher's Book we give an appendix on points of syntax that have not been covered in Part III; where such points, e.g. the use of **quominus** and **quin**, occur in the text, they are simply glossed. There is a further appendix on the Roman calendar. Cicero's letters contain many dates, which are always glossed since we do not think students should have to master the cumbersome Roman calendar in detail. This appendix will enable teachers to give students as much explanation as they think proper. Finally, we supply a sample exercise on each author – together with answers – which is intended to be comparable with the kind of exercise set for the GCSE examination in the UK.

The transition from adapted Latin to unadapted texts is always traumatic and many courses fail at this point. We hope that the grounding in the historical and cultural background provided in the first three parts and the introduction of a considerable amount of undoctored Latin in Part III will make this transition easier. Since Caesar's Latin is considerably easier than that of Cicero, teachers might like to use Caesar's *Commentaries* as the first continuous text to be read by their students.

Commentary

Cover: this delicate fresco portrait of a meditative young girl holding tablets and a pen was discovered at Pompeii and dates from about the middle of the first century AD. It is popularly known as a portrait of Sappho, the Greek poetess. The luminous eyes, the luxuriant curling hair and the fine hair-net add to the impression of beauty and grace. Michael Grant remarks that 'here the artist is more interested in brushwork than in psychology or physical realism'. Do your students agree? (National Archaeological Museum, Naples)
Frontispiece: this rectangular cinerary urn with bucrania (ox skulls, linked with garlands), fruit and nuts, and birds catching insects, dates from the first decades of the first century AD. (Archaeological Museum, Venice)

Cicero

The extracts from Cicero form a continuous biography in which the gaps are filled by the running commentary that introduces each passage. The first three, dealing with his early years, are drawn from speeches and philosophical works but from 68 BC, when his surviving correspondence begins, we use little except his letters. These letters cannot be understood without a knowledge of their historical context, and so the commentary on Cicero in the Reader is considerably longer than that on the other authors; likewise, in the Teacher's Book, where we expand this commentary, more space is given to Cicero than to any of the other authors.

The letters vary considerably in style and linguistic difficulty; for instance, when Cicero writes to Pompey (p. 22) his style is rhetorical and rather pompous; when he writes to his brother Quintus describing the riot in the Forum at Milo's trial (p. 30), he gives an unadorned and fast-moving narrative. He often uses colloquial idiom, omitting verbs, for instance.

Your students may find the letters difficult to start with (for this reason we suggest above that you may want to use the Caesar as their first introduction to a continuous text), but we believe that the generous glossing and, above all, the interest of the content of the letters will enable them to surmount these difficulties. The correspondence of Cicero gives a unique insight both into the character of one of the most important and

fascinating characters of ancient times and into events of great historical significance.

Some useful books:

W. W. How: *Cicero: Select Letters*, Oxford
D. R. Shackleton Bailey: *Cicero: Select Letters*, Cambridge
D. Stockton: *Cicero: A Political Biography*, Oxford
D. Stockton: *Thirty-five Letters of Cicero*, Oxford
Ronald Syme: *The Roman Revolution*, Oxford

1 The young Cicero

de Legibus 2.1.2–3; *Brutus* 306; *pro Plancio* 65; *ad Att.* 1.5.2, 7–8; 1.2

de Legibus 2.1.2–3

Cicero began *de Legibus* in 52 BC; three books survive but it seems to have consisted originally of five. It is cast in dialogue form, the speakers being Cicero himself, Atticus and Cicero's brother Quintus.
1 **his in locis**: Arpinum was a small hill-town in the territory of the Volsci. The Romans captured it in 305–303 BC after the Second Samnite War and gave it *civitas sine suffragio* (citizenship without the vote). After the Social War it became a *municipium*, i.e. a self-governing city with full rights of Roman citizenship.
4–5 **praesertim hoc tempore anni**: what time of year? Cicero might mean spring, when everything is at its most beautiful (**amoenitatem ... hanc sequor**), or he might mean summer, when the heat at Rome was intolerable and the climate unhealthy; then he would want to escape to the health-giving hills (**salubritatem hanc sequor**).
5–6 **raro autem licet**: Cicero never stopped working. Apart from politics, he was continually active in the law-courts (fifty-eight of his speeches survive; another forty-eight are recorded but lost). When the political situation imposed on him a rest from politics, he wrote works on rhetoric and philosophy.
10 **hic sacra**: these were the private religious rites of the family. They centred round the worship of Vesta (goddess of the hearth) and the Lares (the guardian spirits of the family) and the Penates (spirits of the store cupboard).
10–11 **hic sacra, hic genus, hic maiorum multa**

vestigia: as Cicero speaks of his birthplace, his emotions rise and he uses a characteristic rhetorical figure, a tricolon (three units, here noun phrases) in asyndeton (i.e. with no connecting particle), with anaphora (i.e. an emphatic word repeated at the beginning of each unit (**hic**)).

11 **quid plura?**: supply, e.g., **dicam**. 'Why should I say more?' = 'In short, to sum up'. Cicero frequently uses this expression.

15 **scito**: archaic imperative of **scio** = 'know that!'. Cicero is very fond of this word.

15–16 **in animo ac sensu meo** = 'in the feelings of my mind', an example of hendiadys (= one thing expressed by two words).

17 **ille sapientissimus vir**: the reference is to *Odyssey* 5. Odysseus was generally cited as an example of cunning rather than wisdom.

Brutus 306

Brutus (also called *de Claris Oratoribus*) is a work on rhetoric in which Cicero surveys the the past century of oratory; written in 46 BC, it was dedicated to Brutus.

Cicero's introduction to the civil law was by apprenticeship to Mucius Scaevola; in the next generation, rhetorical schools had sprung up and would-be lawyers began their studies by attending one of these. In our society apprenticeship was for long the rule in many spheres but is now being largely replaced by academic study. You might discuss with your students which system they think is better.

19 **in iuris civilis studio**: *ius civile* had developed continuously from the publication of the Twelve Tables of the Law (450 BC), which laid down principles based on the *mos maiorum*. These principles were interpreted and reinterpreted by experts in the law (*iurisprudentes*) for generation after generation, and so *iurisprudentes* had important functions in both advising litigants on procedure and in giving *responsa* to questions on the law put by individuals, magistrates or judges. Quintus Mucius Scaevola (consul 95 BC) was the leading *iurisconsultus* of his generation and published the first systematic treatise on the *ius civile*.

25–6 **in quo hoc ... commorabar ... quod**: Cicero's use of the demonstratives **hic** and **is** referring forward to **ut** or **quod** is extremely common and will undoubtedly confuse your students to start with. It is worth spending some time on the first examples of this idiom that you meet.

pro Plancio 65

Gnaeus Plancius was elected aedile in 55 BC but was prosecuted for using corrupt electoral methods. The prosecution made a digression on the incorruptibility of

Laterensis, the candidate whom Plancius had beaten at the polls, and on his high standards as governor of Cyrene. Cicero says all this is quite irrelevant to the case, even if true. 'In the bustle of life at Rome it is almost impossible to attend to what goes on in the provinces.' He then proceeds to illustrate this from his own quaestorship in Sicily twenty years before.

It is an example of Cicero's great skill in keeping the jury amused when he was afraid they might become bored; he tells the story against himself with a splendid lightness of touch. You might discuss with your students the tone of the passage. Is he being boastful? How would the jury have reacted? At what point does it become clear that he is being funny?

36 **sic tum existimabam**: **sic** looks forward to the following accusative and infinitive.

37–41 **frumenti ... in me inauditi**: in praising his conduct as quaestor Cicero uses an elaborate tricolon with asyndeton: 1 what he did for Rome (**frumenti ... miseram**); 2 his relations with the different classes in his district of Sicily (**negotiatoribus ... diligentissimus**); 3 the honours given him by the Sicilians (**excogitati ... inauditi**). No doubt the jury would have smiled at the eulogy Cicero makes on himself; they were meant to.

41 **hac spe**: this looks forward to the **ut** clause, which expresses consequence: 'with such hope that I thought ...'.

42 **ultro**: 'beyond'; it is often used idiomatically, especially with verbs of offering, giving etc., to mean 'beyond what one would expect'. Cicero hoped that the Roman people would now further his political career ('offer him everything') without any efforts on his part.

47 **num quid esset novi**: 'whether there was anything of new' = 'whether there was any news'.

Cicero continues: 'But this did me more good than if everyone had then congratulated me. For after this I realized that the Roman people had rather poor hearing but very sharp eyes and I stopped worrying about what men would hear about me and saw that from then on they should see me before them everyday; I lived before their eyes, I haunted the Forum.' Certainly, from then on Cicero never left Rome for long if he could help it.

ad Atticum 1.5.2, 7–8

The marriage between Quintus Cicero and Atticus' sister Pomponia had been arranged by Cicero himself, according to Cornelius Nepos (*Life of Atticus* 5: *eas nuptias M. Cicero consiliarat*). The marriage took place probably in 69 BC and must have been unhappy from the start, seeing that this letter was written in the following year. Cicero's attempts to smooth things over and bring about a reconciliation were not successful, as a letter written to Atticus in May 51 BC shows (*ad Att.*

5.1.3). Cicero and his brother Quintus had been staying at Arpinum from where they journeyed with their families to another villa:

> The next day we set out from Arpinum. We had lunch at Quintus' estate at Arcinum. You know the farm. When we got there, Quintus said with the greatest courtesy, 'Pomponia, you invite the women, I'll fetch the men.' [They were inviting the estate workers and their wives to lunch.] Nothing, I thought, could have been more charming and not only in his words but also in the feelings expressed on his face. But she said, in our hearing, 'I'm a visitor then in my own house.' This, I think, because Statius had gone ahead to organize lunch for us. Then Quintus said to me, 'There you are, that's how I suffer every day.' I hid my discomfort. We all took our places at table, except for her, but Quintus sent food out to her from the table. She refused it. In short, no one, it seemed to me, could have been gentler than my brother, no one rougher than your sister, and I omit a great deal which upset me more than Quintus himself.

Despite such quarrels the marriage lasted until 44 BC, when Quintus divorced her.

54 is qui deberet: 'such as it should be'; note the use of the subjunctive; where the correlatives **is ... qui** are used, if the reference of the demonstrative is definite ('the man who ...'), the indicative is used in the relative clause; if the reference is indefinite or generic ('the sort of man who ...'), the subjunctive is used in the relative clause. So, in the next sentence, **eas litteras ... quibus ... placarem**: 'such a letter by which I might placate ...'. Here the relative clause is generic but also expresses purpose. We would simply say: 'a letter to placate him'. (see also Appendix 1, p. 86).

59 Epiroticam emptionem: Atticus' estate in Epirus was at Buthrotum.

ad Atticum 1.2

71 tuo adventu nobis opus est maturo: Atticus had gone to Athens in 85 BC, ostensibly to study but, more likely, to avoid being caught up in civil war. He stayed there for twenty years (hence his *cognomen* Atticus), and only returned in 65 BC to help Cicero in his election campaign. From then on he was frequently in Rome offering help and advice to Cicero.

Some questions for your students: What evidence is there that Cicero wrote this letter in a hurry? What do you think of his plan to defend Catiline? What light does the letter throw on the working of (a) Roman justice and (b) Roman elections?

Illustrations

p. 9: this fine bust of a thoughtful and anxious Cicero dates from the first century BC. (Vatican Museums, Rome)

p. 10: the modern town of Arpino has a population of some 7,500 and is built on two hills.

p. 11: in this *lararium* from the house of the Vettii at Pompeii, the *paterfamilias* is in the centre, making an offering to the Lares who stand on either side of him holding drinking horns. (Alternatively, the man in the toga may represent the *genius* of the family.) Beneath, the sacred serpent is about to consume an offering laid out for it. The spirits of the dead were thought to make their appearance in the form of serpents. (Since serpents live in holes in the ground, they have since very early times been thought of as vehicles for the spirits of the dead.)

p. 12: this bronze statue of a togaed orator (known in Italian as the *Arringatore*) is famous for the arresting pose. It is an Etruscan work of the fourth or third century BC. The purple stripe is clearly visible. (Archaeological Museum, Florence)

p. 15: this fine *peristylium* is from the great Roman villa at Oplontis south of Naples, between Pompeii and Herculaneum. Dating from the first century BC, it is thought to have been the villa of Poppaea, the second wife of Nero.

p. 17: this photograph shows the view from the Castello di Baia, a sixteenth-century fort built above the ancient town of Baiae. We look down to Cape Misenum. At 155 m high, this cape looks so much like an artificial mound that it is traditionally thought of as the burial-place of Misenus, Aeneas' trumpeter (hence the name). Here lived Caius Marius, the fabulously wealthy Lucullus and the emperor Tiberius, who died there in AD 37. Misenum became one of the principal naval bases under Augustus (with Ravenna)

2 Consulship, exile and return

in Cat. 1.1; *ad Fam.* 5.7.2–3; *ad Att.* 2.19.2–3, 3.19.3; *ad Fam.* 14.2.1, 2, 4; *ad Att.* 4.1.4–5, 8; 4.3.2–3; *ad Q.F.* 2.3.2; *ad Fam.* 7.5, 7.7; *ad Q.F.* 2.15.4–5

in Catilinam 1.1

Our accounts of Catiline's conspiracy come from sources that are heavily biased – Cicero himself and Sallust (*Bellum Catilinae*) – and the facts are in dispute. But it seems certain that after his rejection at the polls in July 63 BC Catiline resorted to desperate measures, planning to make an armed uprising in Rome on 28 October and attempting to raise an army in Etruria.

Cicero learnt of this from an informer; he eventually convinced the senate of the danger and on 21 October they passed the *senatus consultum ultimum*, which authorized Cicero to take necessary precautions. Catiline was still at large in the city and now planned to assassinate Cicero and start the uprising. Cicero was forewarned; he escaped assassination and summoned the senate (7 November). He denounced Catiline, who had the nerve to attend the meeting in an attempt to bluff his way out, to his face. Cicero's speech was a masterpiece of emotive invective but contained little hard evidence against Catiline. Catiline hurriedly left the senate and fled that night to join the forces that his lieutenant Manlius was raising in Etruria.

Cicero's introduction to his denunciation of Catiline is highly rhetorical. He begins with three rhetorical questions in asyndeton; the second includes the emotive word **furor**, as common in this speech of Cicero as it is in Virgil's *Aeneid*; the third includes two highly emotive words, separated for emphasis: **effrenata** and **audacia**. The second sentence has five parallel units in asyndeton with anaphora (each introduced by **nihil**); the last of these is the most emphatic, a climax in which he appeals to the very audience before him. If you wish to discuss with your students Cicero's rhetorical skill, this brief passage gives ample scope.

ad Familiares 5.7.2–3

In following the careers of Caesar and Cicero, we are apt to forget that it was Pompey who dominated the politics of this period. The commands he had been given, against the pirates by the *Lex Gabinia* in 67 BC and in the East by the *Lex Manilia* in 66 BC, were unprecedented in the powers devolved upon him. In both commands he had been brilliantly successful, showing himself the greatest general and administrator of his time. He had annihilated the pirates, who had controlled the Mediterranean for many years, in three months, and after finally defeating Mithridates, he had entirely reorganized the East, from the Black Sea in the north to Syria in the south. Although he was absent from Rome from 66 to 62 BC, he overshadowed the scene from afar.

Cicero had consistently supported Pompey when the *optimates* opposed him. Ever since as praetor in 66 BC he had spoken in favour of the *Lex Manilia*, Cicero had hoped to make a political alliance with Pompey and guide him down the path of constitutional opposition to the excesses of the *nobiles*, but Pompey was always unresponsive; he had made no acknowledgement of Cicero's achievements as consul, which the latter found particularly wounding, and in April he wrote the following letter, which makes his hopes and feelings crystal clear. Cicero was still glowing with the memory of his glorious consulship and the extravagant language in which he depicts his success would hardly have appealed to Pompey. It is not surprising that when Pompey returned to Rome, Cicero found him cold.

11 **illud non dubito quin ...**: for **quin**, see Appendix 1, pp. 86.

14 **amicitia**: this word means more than the English friendship; it is often used of political alliance.

15 **necessitudinis**: **necessitudo** = a close relationship of family or friendship, intimacy. It is a remarkably strong word for Cicero to use here.

21–2 **Africanus ... Laelium**: Laelius (consul 140 BC), called *sapiens* because of his devotion to Stoic philosophy, was the leader of the Scipionic circle, the group of brilliant philhellenists that Scipio Aemilianus gathered round him (they included the dramatist Terence, the satirist Lucilius and the historian Polybius). Scipio, a liberal in politics, relied on him greatly for advice. One can understand how Cicero would have longed to play Laelius to Pompey's Scipio, but Pompey was no Scipio; brilliant as he was as a general and administrator, he was a bungler in politics with no firm principles.

The letter to Pompey is rather formal in style, containing a large number of doublets of the sort we find in his speeches. You might ask your students to compare the style of this letter with one of those to Atticus, e.g. that on p. 18.

ad Atticum 2.19.2–3

In December 60 BC Caesar sent his confidential secretary Balbus to make overtures to Cicero: 'He said that Caesar would use the advice of Pompey and myself in all matters and would make efforts to unite Crassus with Pompey. This means for me a close alliance with Pompey, if I accept it, and also with Caesar, a return to favour with my enemies, peace with the masses, tranquillity in my old age' (*ad Att*. 2.3.3). But Cicero bravely rejected this tempting offer and could only sit on the sidelines, watching the situation deteriorate.

Caesar began his year as consul trying to cooperate with the senate; he brought before them a moderate land law, providing land for Pompey's veterans. When the senate rejected his proposal, he took it to the people; the law was passed in the *concilium plebis* with illegal violence in the teeth of strong opposition from Caesar's colleague in the consulship, Bibulus. He then carried a measure to confirm Pompey's arrangements in the East, thus completing his bargain with Pompey. Bibulus shut himself in his house, posting notices to his door to say that Caesar's measures were illegal, since he had observed the omens and they were unfavourable.

By June Cicero sees no hope: *tenemur undique*

neque iam quominus serviamus recusamus ('we are hemmed in on every side and now cannot rebel against our slavery', *ad Att.* 2.17.1). In July he wrote again to Atticus in despair at the situation.

34 nostra miseria tu es magnus: this was not the only line that seemed to the people to point to Pompey; Cicero continues: 'He said amidst shouts from the whole theatre: "The time will come when you will bitterly lament the same virtue." One might think that verses of this sort had been written by an enemy of Pompey for the occasion.'

36 Curio filius: Curio the younger at this time won popularity by opposing Caesar openly but later, as tribune for 50 BC, he was bought over by Caesar and supported him, vetoing all attempts by the senate to recall Caesar from Gaul.

Cicero had had the courage to attack the triumvirs publicly in a speech in March (*de Dom.* 16.41); Caesar could not afford to leave him active in Rome when he departed for Gaul. He bore him no ill-will and offered him several chances of avoiding trouble, even a post as legate on his staff. When Cicero rejected these overtures, Caesar resorted to sterner measures. He sanctioned the adoption of Publius Claudius Pulcher, a member of a distinguished patrician family, and an old enemy of Cicero, into a plebeian family, which enabled him to stand for the tribunate. Claudius changed his name to Clodius (the plebeian spelling), was duly elected and was given by Caesar the task of keeping an eye on his interests in Rome and getting rid of Cicero.

Before Caesar had even left for Gaul Clodius introduced a programme of popular legislation and followed this up with an enactment aimed at Cicero, that any one who had put Roman citizens to death without trial should be outlawed. The triumvirs refused to come to his help and although he was supported by most of the senate and knights, Cicero felt that he had no option but to flee. On the very day he left Rome, Clodius' bill was passed and he immediately followed it with another formally declaring Cicero an outlaw. His goods were forfeit and both his town house and his villas at Formiae and Tusculum were confiscated and destroyed. As soon as Caesar had heard that Cicero was safely out of the way he left for Gaul.

ad Atticum 3.19.3

In exile Cicero wrote a series of letters to Atticus asking for his help and advice (twenty-six letters survive from when he set out for exile in March 58 BC until February 57 BC, six months before his recall). He seesaws between hope and despair, more often despair.

The letter we quote is written in a rhetorical style, which comes naturally to Cicero in moments of strong emotion. He uses tricola with anaphora: **si ... si ... si ...**; doublets: **oro et obsecro, carissimis iucundissimisque**; the strongly emotive word **misericordia**.

38–9 omnibus ... rebus: literally: 'all the most ample, dearest and most delightful things' i.e. 'all that I enjoyed in such ample measure, all that I most valued and delighted in' (Shackleton Bailey). He means not only the material advantages of his situation (grand house, country villas etc.) but his influential position as a senior statesman, his *dignitas*.

45 xvi Kal. Oct. = **ante diem xvi Kalendas Octobres**, i.e. the sixteenth day before 1 October. On this and all other dates, see Appendix 2.

ad Familiares 14.2.1, 2, 4

The following month he wrote a letter to Terentia which is equally sad but which is written in a less rhetorical style; it seems to come straight from the heart. Students might be asked to compare the style of the two letters.

ad Atticum 4.1.4–5, 8

Cicero recounts the story of his triumphant return with justifiable pride; he knows that Atticus will have heard all about it by now but cannot resist telling him how enthusiastic his reception was.

74 comitiis centuriatis: the three principal assemblies of the people were the *comitia centuriata*, the *comitia populi tributa* and the *concilium plebis*. The first elected the major magistrates (consuls and praetors) and passed laws (*leges*); the people voted by units called centuries into which they were distributed according to their wealth, so that the votes of richer citizens were worth more than those of the poorer. The second elected the minor magistrates (aediles and quaestors) and could enact laws; the people voted by the tribes in which they were registered on assuming the *toga virilis*. The *concilium plebis* elected the ten *tribuni plebis* and enacted *plebiscita*, which since 287 BC had the same validity as *leges*. Patricians were excluded from this assembly (hence Clodius had to be adopted into a plebeian family before he could become a tribune).

78 infima plebe: literally 'the lowest plebs'; although *plebs* properly means the whole citizen body of the people of Rome except for the patricians, it is often used to mean the 'masses', sometimes with connotations of contempt; so Cicero speaks of the *misera ac ieiuna plebecula* ('the wretched starving mob', *ad Att.* 1.16).

86 praesentibus occulte irasci: three days after his return to Rome Cicero proposed in the senate that Pompey should be given an extraordinary command with wide powers to manage the corn supply (there was a serious shortage of corn in Rome). His proposal was carried with opposition from the more extreme *optimates*, who were both jealous and nervous of Pompey. By his first intervention in politics on his return Cicero was attempting once again to form an *amicitia* with Pompey; in doing so he both alienated the extreme *optimates* and alerted Caesar, who was winning a series of brilliant victories in Gaul, to the danger of a split in the triumvirate.

ad Atticum 4.3.2–3

An extraordinary feature of the next four years was the uncontrolled rampaging of Clodius. His gangs ruled the streets; egged on by the more extreme *optimates*, he caused havoc, using undisguised violence against his enemies. Cicero remained one of his principal targets.
93 **vicatim ambire**: 'he goes round street by street'; **vicus** means properly a block of houses bounded on all sides by streets, but came to mean a district or ward, and then a village. **ambio** means 'I go round' and then 'I go round canvassing for votes' (hence **ambitio** = 'ambition'). The phrase probably means: 'He is going round the wards trying to win support.'
93–4 **servis ... spem libertatis ostendere**: to enrol the support of slaves was the last refuge of the desperate.

ad Quintum Fratrem 2.3.2

By the following February, when Clodius prosecuted Milo *de vi*, Pompey was estranged from Crassus, who was, he thought, encouraging Clodius to attack him, and he decided to support Milo in court. The letter quoted shows clearly how law and order had given way to mob violence.

The passage illustrates Cicero's ability to write a lucid and exciting narrative. He uses no rhetorical devices. Events follow each other in quick succession with just enough detail to bring the scene before his reader's mind. At the end things are moving quickly; the style becomes breathless and staccato as he uses a succession of short sentences, often omiting verbs.

By April 56 BC Pompey had not only quarrelled with Crassus but was becoming jealous of Caesar, whose victories in Gaul were beginning to eclipse his own in the East. Cicero thought that there was a real chance of breaking up the triumvirate and on 5 April attacked some of Caesar's legislation in a speech in the senate. Caesar reacted at once; he summoned Pompey and Crassus to a conference at Luca where the triumvirate was renewed with prizes for all three: Caesar's command in Gaul was extended for five years, Pompey and Crassus were to be consuls the following year (55 BC), after which Crassus was to be governor of

Syria and Pompey to be governor of Spain with the option of staying in Rome and administering the province through lieutenants. Cicero was brought to heel and forced to make a speech in which he supported Caesar (*de Provinciis Consularibus*).

Although he undertook several important cases in the law-courts in 55 and 54 BC, his letters show that he spent much time moving between his different country villas while he was busy writing his great work on oratory (*de Oratore*, in three books, completed in November 55 BC). The following year he started a work on politics, which he later developed into the the six books *de Republica* and the three *de Legibus*.

ad Familiares 7.5

Caesar always admired Cicero and even felt some affection for him despite their political differences. Cicero, although humiliated by his enforced subservience to the triumvirs, did not hesitate to write to Caesar on behalf of a promising young friend who had asked for his help. But the letter has a certain stiffness and artificiality; Cicero goes over the top both in his protestations of friendship and in his lavish commendation of Trebatius. You might ask your students what they feel about this.

ad Familiares 7.7

This short letter is a masterpiece; Cicero administers a rebuke to Trebatius, without being offensive, on his failure to answer letters and makes it quite clear that if Trebatius does not succeed, it will be his own fault. But he spices this unwelcome message with humour.

You might ask your students to make a list of the reproaches which are the 'subtext' of this letter and to show how Cicero succeeds in rebuking Trebatius without hurting his feelings too much.
130 **nihil ... neque auri neque argenti**: the double negative for emphasis is characteristic of colloquial Latin. Britian did in fact have some mineral resources – gold in Wales, lead in the Mendips, tin in Cornwall – but Caesar's raids into Britain did not bring him anywhere near them.

ad Quintum Fratrem 2.15.4–5

Quintus Cicero had transferred to Caesar's staff from that of Pompey early in 54 BC. He was given command of a legion and, if your students read the Caesar extracts before the Cicero, you might remind them that by the time he got this letter, he would have been heavily engaged in the advance from Kent to the Thames, which was not achieved without casualties. The following year he commanded the winter quarters of a legion stationed in Gaul and gallantly defended his camp against the attacks of the rebellious Gauls, earning high praise from Caesar (see pp. 90–101 of the Reader).

In the previous two paragraphs of this letter Cicero says how busy he is in the law-courts and promises not to give offence to Caesar or his supporters. One might certainly feel that he should have started by saying how relieved he was that his brother had reached Britain safely.

140 **reliqua**: 'the rest', i.e. the campaigns that would follow their successful landing. Cicero did not expect much trouble here; like others, he underestimated the determination and courage of the Britons.

142 **materiam scribendi**: Cicero seems to think that the most important aspect of his brother's active service in remotest Britain was the material it would provide for writing. You might ask your students what they think of this.

146–7 **neget ... legisse**: Caesar was no mean critic of literature, and as an orator was second only to Cicero himself. Could there be a touch of irony in his remark that 'as for the first part I've never read anything better even in Greek'? Cicero continues: 'The rest, he says, is a little slipshod (for this is the word he uses). Tell me truly, is it the matter or the style he does not like?'

We think of Caesar as the ruthless military man. You might like to discuss with your students the different picture of his character that emerges from this letter – a highly civilized man discussing literature with Quintus in his tent in the evening.

In 53 BC the disorder in Rome was such that the consular elections were repeatedly blocked by tribunes. Eventually in spring 52 BC, after the riots that followed Clodius' murder and the burning of the senate house, the senate declared martial law and instructed Pompey to provide for the safety of the state (the *senatus consultum ultimum*). But disorders continued and Pompey was finally appointed sole consul and began to clear up the mess. When Milo was prosecuted for the murder of Clodius in April, Pompey was determined that he should not be acquitted; he packed the court house with soldiers and Cicero abandoned his attempt to deliver a defence.

Illustrations

p. 21: this famous painting by Cesare Maccari (1840–1919) hangs in the Palazzo Madama in Rome, which has been the seat of the Italian Senate since 1871.
p. 25: this statuette of a tragic actor is of ivory coloured blue with the sleeves striped blue and yellow. The actor, whose mouth can be seen through his mask and who is wearing high, stilt-like shoes, is playing the part of a woman. (Musée du Petit Palais, Paris)
p. 28: a page from a mid-fifteenth-century manuscript of Cicero, written in formal humanist script. Note the differences between the text we have printed (p. 26, l. 67 and following) and that of the manuscript (MS.Add.c. 139, Bodleian Library, Oxford).
p. 29: this gate is not the Porta Capena, which has not survived, but the Porta Appia (now called the Porta San Sebastiano), the most imposing gateway in the Aurelian wall of Rome, which was built in the second half of the third century AD. The wall was 19 km in perimeter and had 300 towers and 14 main gates. It was punctuated by 2,000 small windows. The two towers in the photograph are mediaeval.
p. 31: the ruins of Domitian's palace on the side of the Palatine hill, which rises south of the Forum to a height of 51 m.
p. 35: the senate house (curia) was begun by Sulla in 80 BC and was destroyed by fire when Clodius' supporters burnt his body in the Forum (January, 52 BC). Rebuilding was begun by Julius Caesar in 44 BC. Marble originally covered the brick face in the lower area, with stucco above.

3 Governor of Cilicia

ad Att. 5.16, 5.20.2–3; *ad Fam.* 2.12, 8.14.1–3, 16.1

ad Atticum 5.16

Pompey, in an attempt to lessen political corruption, had put through a law that there should be a five-year interval between office in Rome and holding a provincial governorship. The senate decreed that, to fill the gap this caused, all qualified ex-magistrates who had not governed a province should do so now. Cicero was allotted the province of Cilicia, one of the remotest in the empire, bordering on the Parthian empire, a danger spot, for ever since Crassus' disastrous defeat at Carrhae two years before, the Parthians were expected to attack at any moment.

2 **publicanorum tabellarii**: the letter carriers of the *publicani* provided the only channel of communication with Rome for those who were overseas; they were freedmen or slaves employed for this purpose by the companies in Rome. There was no official postal service until Augustus organized the *cursus publicus* for official dispatches.

6 **maxima exspectatione**: reports of Cicero's appointment must have gone ahead of his arrival, and the provincials who had been so fleeced by his predecessor Appius Claudius Pulcher, elder brother of Clodius, must have been looking forward hopefully to

his arrival.

10–11 nullus fit sumptus in nos: governors and their staff hoped to make a fortune out of their term of office. Catullus on his return from service on the governor's staff in Bithynia was asked how much he had made out the province. He answered that his governor was such a b— that he hadn't made a penny (Catullus 10, see p. 136 of the Reader). No doubt, if he had served under Cicero, he would have said the same. Provincials had means of redress through the extortion court in Rome (*quaestio de rebus repetundis*) and many governors whose conduct had been particularly scandalous were prosecuted before it. But the cases were often decided not on their merits but on political grounds (it may be remembered that Cicero thought of defending Catiline, 'although his guilt is clear as daylight', in order to get his help in his campaign for the consulship) and it was not easy to secure a conviction.

ad Atticum 5.20.2–3

Cicero writes to Atticus (December 50 BC) in high spirits to recount his military successes, achieved the previous October.

25 Tarsum veni: Tarsus, the birthplace of St Paul, was perhaps the most important city in Cilicia and became its capital in the next century.

29–30 imperatores appellati sumus: the title *imperator* was first conferred by his troops on L. Aemilius Paullus in 189 BC and by the late republic it was regularly awarded to successful generals in the field. It was not a permanent title but had to be surrendered by its holders when they reentered the city of Rome and returned to civilian life. The first man to hold the title permanently was Julius Caesar. From 38 BC Octavian made it part of his *praenomen* and it came to denote supreme power, so that on coins and in official inscriptions the emperor's titles begin, e.g., *Imp. Caesar divi filius Augustus.*

31 apud Issum Alexander: the reference to Alexander no doubt made Atticus smile, and it was intended to.

34–5 timor Parthis iniectus est: Cicero's success had consequences more important than the victory itself, resulting in the withdrawal of the Parthian army from Antioch. Cicero went on to capture Pindenissus, a heavily fortified native stronghold, which he took after a siege of fifty-seven days. In his letter to Atticus, Cicero, pleased as he is at his victory, is inclined to make light of his success.

It seems extraordinary to us that Cicero, a leading barrister, statesman and philosopher, who had seen no military service except as a very junior officer in his early youth, should suddenly, at the age of fifty-one, have been given command of an army in a dangerous province and should have successfully conducted military operations. He was, of course, helped by his *legati*, chosen no doubt for their military experience; these included his brother Quintus, who had commanded a legion under Caesar and fought with great distinction in Gaul. But you might have a lively discussion with your students on this topic.

ad Familiares 2.12

Marcus Caelius Rufus (born 82 BC) was a brilliant but rather unstable young man. When he had assumed the *toga virilis*, he became for three years a pupil of Cicero, who admired his ability. But he then broke away from Cicero and became entangled with Catiline. It was perhaps he who became the lover of Clodia after she had thrown over Catullus (see p. 124 of the Reader) and when after two years he had tired of her, there was a furious quarrel, which ended in Clodia's engineering a prosecution of Caelius for riot. The charges were flimsy and the defence, led by Cicero, secured an acquittal (see pp. 124–6). Caelius then continued his political career. He became tribune in 52 BC and helped Milo in his struggles against Clodius.

Before Cicero went to Cilicia, he asked Caelius to keep him in touch with events in Rome; he wrote Cicero seventeen letters (*ad Familiares* 8), which well illustrate his character; they are light-hearted, amusing and cynical and show a keen insight into political events; as Cicero says, he could not have had a better correspondent.

His subsequent career shows the volatility of his nature and his cynical self-interestedness. In the civil war he chose to throw in his lot with Caesar, a choice foreshadowed at the end of the next extract (*ad Fam.* 8.14.3). But in 48 BC as praetor he proposed a programme of radical reforms and when Trebonius, the *praetor urbanus*, opposed him, he started a riot and drove Trebonius out of the Forum. The senate then deposed him from office. He fled to South Italy to join Milo, who was now trying to raise a revolt against Caesar. The revolt was put down by Caesarian soldiers and Caelius was killed in the battle.

37 sollicitus ... eram de rebus urbanis: Cicero had every reason to be worried about affairs at Rome. As the letter Caelius wrote to him three months later shows, civil war now seemed inevitable. The issue was the date of Caesar's recall from Gaul, which would result in his laying down his command and losing his army. If he did this before he was elected to a second consulship, he would have been prosecuted and ruined. All the senate's proposals to recall Caesar were vetoed by Curio, now tribune, who had begun the year as an opponent of Caesar but who was now in his pay. At the

Quinquatrus (l. 38) Curio was agitating on Caesar's behalf.

43 annuum munus: Cicero had arrived in Cilicia at the end of July and he was determined to leave the moment the year was up, whether his successor had arrived or not. He stayed in Tarsus until 17 July and sailed from the port of Sida in Pamphylia. Sailing via Rhodes, Ephesus and Piraeus, he reached Patrae on 2 November, where he had to leave his secretary Tiro, who was ill (see *ad Fam.* 16.1, p. 42). He was held up by storms at Corfu for a fortnight and did not reach Brundisium until 24 November. He did not go straight to Rome since he was still hoping for a triumph, but he met Pompey in Campania on 11 December, who warned him that civil war was now inevitable. His whole journey from Cilicia had lasted five months.

ad Familiares 8.14.1–3

Caelius wrote in early August and the letter caught up with Cicero on 14 October at Piraeus. It must have confirmed his worst fears. It was all very well for Caelius to be amused by the reaction of Domitius when he was not elected augur, but the second paragraph contained an acute analysis of the political situation which showed that now there was no hope of avoiding civil war.

59–60 quo propius ... eo clarius: on comparative clauses, see Appendix 1, pp. 85–6.

66–9 in hac discordia ... accessuros: Caelius had probably already made up his mind to go over to Caesar; he admits that Pompey will have more respectable support, but Caesar's army is incomparably better and so the only safe course is to join him.

ad Familiares 16.1

We do not know anything about Tiro's origins but we are told that 'he had been liberally educated from his earliest years' (Aulus Gellius: *Noctes Atticae* 6.3.8); he was given his freedom when he was still very young, and when we first meet him in Cicero's letters, he seems more like a family friend than a servant. He began to collect Cicero's letters while Cicero was still alive and wrote several books about his master and also books on the Latin language. Cicero need not have been so concerned about his health; he lived to be ninety-nine.

The letter would give you the opportunity to discuss the relations between slaves and freedmen and their masters.

74–5 qui a te discesserim: on the use of the subjunctive, see Appendix 1, p. 86.

73 magni ... interest: 'it is of great importance': the impersonal verb **interest** = 'it makes a difference', 'it is important'; it is here used with a genitive of value (**magni**).

Illustrations

p. 39: this dramatic picture of the Battle of Issus (333 BC), a large floor mosaic (3.42 × 5.92 m) dazzlingly executed in minute tesserae in about 150 BC, is from the House of the Faun at Pompeii. It vividly conveys a ferment of movement and emotion. To the left Alexander, with hair characteristically flying, is a study in concentration. The despairing Darius (centre right) holds out his arm in an eloquent gesture. The horse is front of him is a brilliant example of foreshortening; and note the gorgon Medusa's head on Alexander's breastplate. The composition is thought to be modelled on a fourth-century BC Greek painting, probably by Philoxenos of Eretria. (National Archaeological Museum, Naples)

4 Civil war and death

ad Att. 9.6a, 9.11a1; *ad Fam.* 14.7, 14.20; *ad Att.* 12.15, 13.52; *ad Fam.* 6.15, 9.24.4; *Tusc. Disp.* 1.117; Livy fr. 50

ad Atticum 9.6a

Caesar wrote this letter in March 49 BC while pursuing Pompey to Brundisium. He was in great haste, hoping to catch up with Pompey before he sailed. That he wrote to Cicero at such a time shows how genuinely anxious he was to win his support. Cicero must have sent a copy of this letter to Atticus, along with his reply (see the next extract), which explains how they have survived as part of the *ad Atticum* collection.

4 praeterire ... non potui quin: on **quin**, see Appendix 1, pp. 86.

8 dignitate: a difficult word, which means **1** worth, merit; **2** the importance or authority derived from this merit.

ad Atticum 9.11a1

Cicero replied promptly to Caesar, writing from his villa at Formiae on 19 March. The tone of the letter is chillingly formal, in contrast to that of Caesar, which is warmly affectionate.

Cicero met Caesar on 28 March at Formiae. He described the interview in a letter to Atticus written on 1 April (*ad Att.* 9.18):

Caesar said, 'Come and make proposals for peace.' 'On my own terms?' I said. 'Am I to prescribe to you?' he replied. 'Then I shall say that the senate cannot approve an expedition to Spain or the transport of armies to Greece and I shall express my full sympathy for Pompey.' Then he said, 'That's not what I want said.' 'So I thought,' I replied. In the end he asked me to think things over. So we parted. I don't think he likes me. But I liked myself, which I have not done for a long time.

If Cicero's account is true, he showed considerable courage on this occasion.

ad Familiares 14.7

This letter is full of affection and concern for Terentia and Tullia; he himself was embarking on a course that might end in his death (he knew that Caesar's army was vastly superior to that of Pompey) and he was leaving his loved ones to unknown dangers; Italy might be ravaged by war. It is sad to contrast this letter with the next, written to Terentia the following October.

ad Atticum 12.15

These years saw Cicero struck down by one cruel blow after another in both public and private life. Of all these, the bitterest was the death of his beloved Tullia. His resilience is astounding.

ad Atticum 13.52

Caesar invited himself to dinner, another proof of the affection he felt for Cicero despite the latter's consistent opposition to him. Cicero describes the occasion to Atticus in a light, colloquial style, looking back on it with a mixture of pride and ironical admiration for the way he had pulled it off.

ad Familiares 6.15

Cicero's immediate reaction to the assassination of Caesar was undiluted joy that the republic had been saved from a tyrant. But considering the magnanimous way Caesar had treated Cicero, one can hardly fail to regret the exultant tone of this hastily written note. He wrote in a similar tone to Cassius a year later (ad Fam. 12.4, February 43 BC): vellem Idibus Martiis me ad cenam invitasses; reliquiarum nihil fuisset ('I wish you had invited me to your dinner on the Ides of March; there would have been no left-overs', i.e. Antony would have been assassinated too).

ad Familiares 9.24.4

After the meeting of the senate on 17 March, at which Cicero had taken the lead in proposing an amnesty, he played no part in politics for six months but retired to the country and devoted himself to literature, composing no less than six philosophical works. Cicero had been helpless while Antony was still in Italy but the moment he left for Gaul, he published a pamphlet in which he made a scathing attack on him (2nd Philippic) and then went to Rome to rally senate and people against him (3rd and 4th Philippic, 20 December). He now stood at the head of the republican party and worked ceaselessly, enlisting Octavian to the cause, shaping policy in the senate and writing endless letters to the governors of the provinces to ensure their loyalty.

In the midst of all this hectic activity Cicero found time to write to his friend L. Papirius Paetus, an Epicurean philosopher who kept out of politics. The letter is light in tone; Papirius had written that he had given up entertaining or going to dinner parties. Cicero says this is a mistake; nothing is more suited to the happy life (the highest good for Epicureans) than such parties. He ends: 'See that you keep well; you will achieve this most easily by going out to dinners.' He then adds the paragraph we quote.

Tusculan Disputations 1.117

When Octavian turned against the republican cause and joined forces with Antony, Cicero knew that all that he had fought for was finished and that his own death was imminent. As far as philosophy could help, he had prepared himself for this.

In the passage quoted Cicero echoes the words Socrates addressed to those of the jury who had acquitted him, after he had been condemned to death in 399 BC (Plato: Apology 41d–42):

Let us consider this way too, that we can have high hopes that death is a good. For there are two possibilities: either it is annihilation and the dead man has no sensation of anything, or, as we are told, it is a change and the soul moves its dwelling from this world to another. But if there is no sensation and it is like a dreamless sleep, then death would be a wonderful gain ... for all time seems no more than one night. But if death is like a journey from this world to another and what is said is true, that in that other world are all the dead, what greater good could there be than this? ... But you must be hopeful in the face of death and hang on to this one truth, that nothing evil can happen to the good man, either in life or death, and that the fate of such a man is not neglected by the gods ... But now is the time to leave, for me to die, for you to live, and which of us is going to the better fate, is unknown to all but god.

Livy fragment 50

Plutarch says that Octavian tried to save Cicero from Antony's vengeance, but Antony was implacable (*Life of Antony* 19). He was killed on 9 December 43 BC.

Livy's *History* ran from the foundation of Rome to the death of Drusus (9 BC) in 142 books. Of this immense work only books 1–9 and 21–45 survive entire; of the rest we have only fragments and excerpts. The fragment on Cicero's death is from Book 120.

Illustrations

p. 45: from Trajan's Column. We here reproduce the note of R. L. Dalladay, who took this photograph: 'A crisis has occurred some distance from the army's current position, and with a great sense of urgency the soldiers pack their tents (left) and other belongings into the waiting ships. Trajan, accompanied by *singulares* (his auxiliary bodyguard), is about to board a bireme [a boat with oars at two levels]. They are wearing travelling dress, consisting of cloak and tunic. In the background is probably a legionary fortress, with an amphitheatre outside the walls [a characteristic of Roman forts]. At the far right is the stern of a boat transporting horses – the hindquarters of one and the muzzle of another are just, barely, visible.'

p. 48: the acropolis of Cumae is 78 m high. At the foot is the cave of the Cumaean Sibyl, where Aeneas consulted Apollo's inspired priestess. There is a temple of Apollo half way up the hill and a temple of Jupiter on the summit. 'Here the beauty of the view and the stillness, broken only by the rustle of lizards and the sea, make an indelible impression' (Paul Blanchard, *Blue Guide to Southern Italy*).

p. 52: the coin of the triumvir Marcus Aemilius Lepidus gives him the title *Pon[tifex] Max[imus]* (= High Priest). This was the post to which Antony had him appointed in Caesar's place after the latter's murder. (Octavian, by then called Augustus, took over the title when Lepidus died in 13 or 12 BC.) Octavian is entitled Caesar as Julius Ceasar's adoptive heir. Antony is given the title *Imp[erator]* (= general).

p. 53: the ruins of the rostra, brought forward from the original site in front of the curia during Caesar's restoration in 44 BC. Columns supporting commemorative statues rose from the platform. The first structure was adorned with the rostra (= 'beaks' for ramming) of the ships captured from Antium in 338 BC.

p. 54: the so-called tomb of Cicero, near Gaeta (modern Caieta) in Southern Italy.

The excerpts we have made from Cicero's letters are intended above all to convey something of the character of a man whose works and life had immense influence on later generations. Despite all his faults, his vanity, his volatility, and his occasional complacency, he was a man of courage and principle, a champion of liberty and a great humanist.

You might want to ask your students to write an assessment of his character, with quotations from the letters to support their case. Or, a more limited question, you might ask them to write about his relations with his family and close friends. You might also ask whether they think the cause for which he gave his life was worth it, or was the republic in such a bad way that it had no chance?

Caesar

The extracts from Caesar are considerably longer than those from our other authors, providing two separate but consecutive narratives; the first, from *de Bello Gallico* (*BG*) 4.20 to 5.22, gives Caesar's account of the invasions of Britain in 55 and 54 BC; the second (*BG* 5.26–52) tells the story of the rebellions in Gaul that followed in the winter of 54 BC. The first narrative shows how Britain was opened up to the Roman world and how stoutly the Britons resisted the Roman invaders. The second falls into two parts: in the first, the improvident and despicable behaviour of one of the legionary commanders results in disaster; in the second, victory is snatched from defeat through the heroism of Cicero's brother Quintus.

Teachers may choose to use only one of these two narratives, if they are short of time; and since the Latin of Caesar is considerably easier than that of Cicero, they may prefer to begin by reading the Caesar as the first continuous text their students attempt. We leave Caesar's text unaltered apart from some omissions.

The notes in the Reader give sufficient information to make the narrative intelligible; the commentary in the Teacher's book expands these notes and gives some account of topics not discussed in the Reader. We occasionally suggest questions that teachers may wish to ask their students.

Britain at the time of Caesar's invasion

The whole of Britain was at this time inhabited by Celtic speakers; the tribes of the south spoke Brythonic, the same language as that of the Gauls, from which are descended Welsh, Breton and Cornish. The Britons were grouped in tribes, some large and powerful, others small and weak (there were four kings in Kent alone). They were not, as the Romans thought, woad-painted savages (they painted themselves with woad only for battle), but had a highly developed culture which had at one time stretched from Britain to Asia Minor. A branch of this people had invaded Italy in the fourth century BC and had taken and sacked Rome (387 BC); they had then settled in what is now the north of Italy in the area called Cisalpine Gaul.

Their kingship was elective and the kings were bound to some extent to follow the dictates of their people. There was no individual ownership of land; apart from that set aside for the kings and civil service, land was held in common. There was a professional class of bards, doctors and Druids. The Druids were not only the ministers of the Celtic religion but philosophers, teachers and natural scientists, and they were extremely influential. Britain was the centre of the Druidic religion and young men often came from Gaul to undertake the long and strenuous training, which might last for twenty years; the teaching was oral and involved learning innumerable verses. We know little of the content of their teaching but it included a doctrine of immortality and a strict moral code. The Britons were good astronomers and had a sophisticated calendar which synchronized the lunar and solar year over a five-year period. Finally, the Celts were poets, musicians and superb artists, especially in metalwork.

Relations between the Celts of Britain and those of the continent were close; they had a common language and culture, and several Gallic tribes crossed over to Britain and settled there. The Parisii had arrived in Yorkshire in the third century BC, and more recently the Atrebates, who came from Belgium, had settled in Berkshire, keeping their original name. In 57 BC chiefs of the Bellovaci had fled from Gaul to Britain when threatened by Caesar (*BG* 2.14). Caesar himself says that the south-east of Britain was inhabited by Belgic tribes who had crossed from Gaul and settled there, and that their culture was closely similar to that of the Gauls (*BG* 5.14).

Caesar's ignorance of the geography of Britain and the culture of its inhabitants may seem remarkable, but this ignorance was universal in the Roman world of Caesar's time and thereafter; so Catullus, writing at the very time of Caesar's invasions, describes the Britons as *horribilesque ultimosque Britannos* ('the terrible Britons at the end of the world', 11.12–13) and Virgil describes them as *penitus toto divisos orbe* ('completely cut off from the whole world', *Ecl.* 1.66).

It is worth adding an account of Commius, who played a part in Caesar's invasions of Britain and whose career illustrates the close relations between Gaul and Britain. When Caesar had conquered the Belgic Atrebates in 57 BC, he installed Commius as their king and trusted him as a loyal supporter of the Romans. When he was about to invade Britain in 55 BC, he sent him over to Britain to win over British tribes to the Roman cause (*BG* 4.21). After the successful landing, the Britons sent envoys suing for peace and with them came Commius, who said he had not returned to Caesar sooner because he had been arrested and held by British chieftains (4.27). He brought with him a small force of thirty cavalry, which were to prove useful to Caesar later (4.35). The following year, when Cassivellaunus was forced to seek peace, Caesar used Commius as his go-between (5.22).

Caesar continued to trust Commius and in 53 BC left him with a cavalry force to guard the Rhine crossing while he marched against the Treveri. But in the winter of 53/52 BC Labienus (Caesar's principal subordinate commander) heard that he was inciting the Gauls to revolt; he sent Volusenus to parley with him with orders to try to assassinate him. The attempt failed; Commius was seriously wounded but escaped. When Vercingetorix raised the great revolt (52 BC) and was being besieged at Alesia, Commius was one of the commanders of the vast army that marched to relieve the siege (7.76). After the fall of Alesia and capture of Vercingetorix, Commius fled to Germany (8.21). From there he made his way to Britain and was accepted as king of the British Atrebates in Berkshire; he established a dynasty, being succeeded by his son Tincommius.

By the end of 56 BC Caesar had overrun all Gaul from the Pyrenees to the Rhine and could claim that the whole of this vast area had been subdued (*omni Gallia pacata, BG* 3.27). In April of that year the triumvirate had been renewed and Caesar's command had been extended for five years. If Gaul had now been conquered, how was this extension to be justified? One of Caesar's motives for invading Britain may have been the necessity for finding a further field for military operations which would both justify the extension of his command and, by new conquests, enhance his reputation in Rome. Moreover, although he claimed to have pacified Gaul, in fact he was well aware that the situation was highly volatile and, according to his own account, 'in nearly all the wars in Gaul the Britons had sent help to our enemies' (4.20); and so he could argue that as long as the Britons remained unconquered, there was a danger that they might foment rebellion on the mainland. Lastly, there was the prospect of enriching himself and his army and the state from the booty to be gained from an island that was said to be rich in minerals.

The *Commentaries*

The *Commentarii de Bello Gallico* were a new genre of
Latin literature. No general before Caesar had written
an account of his own campaigns. It is worth
remembering that Caesar was acknowledged in his own
time as an orator second only to Cicero and that the
Commentaries were not his only literary effort; he
wrote three more books of *Commentaries* on the civil
war, an attack on Cato, answering Cicero's lost
pamphlet in praise of Cato, and a work on literary style
called *On Analogy* (the latter two are lost). The
evidence of Cicero's letters (e.g. Cicero's letter to his
brother Quintus in Britain, see p. 32 of the Reader)
confirms that Caesar had a keen interest in literature
and was reckoned a percipient critic. It is therefore not
surprising that he should wish to write an account of his
great victories in Gaul, especially since it would both
enhance his reputation in Rome and justify the
continual expansion of the conquests that he undertook
in the name of the Roman people. It is disputed whether
he published them year by year at the end of the
campaigning season or all together after he had left
Gaul. It seems probable that he wrote them in rough
each year and published them in a revised form later;
the most likely time for this revision would seem to be
after the suppression of the revolt of Vercingetorix
(52 BC), when there were no major campaigns. Their
form, an apparently straight factual account written in
the third person, gives an appearance of objectivity, but
there can be little doubt that he intended to represent
himself as an infallible general undertaking necessary
wars in the interests of the Roman people. They do,
therefore, contain an element of propaganda; it is not
that he can be faulted on any matter of fact, but the facts
are usually presented in the light most favourable to the
author.

   Cicero, after a discussion of Caesar's oratorical
style in the Brutus, goes on to say of the *Commentaries*
(*Brutus* 262):

> Brutus replied, 'His speeches certainly appear to me
> extremely praiseworthy. I have read a number of
> them, and also his *Commentaries* which he
> composed about his deeds.'
>   Atticus answered, 'They are indeed
> praiseworthy; they are like nude statues, upright and
> full of charm, stripped of all the clothing of
> rhetorical ornament ... In history there is nothing
> more pleasing than clear and brilliant brevity.'

Caesar writes in a plain style, in contrast with the
elaborate, often rhetorical, style of Livy, and the
compressed and sometimes difficult style of Tacitus.
Each author suits his style to his end; Caesar intended
his readers to find a straightforward factual account of
his achievements. And so the narrative moves swiftly,
each sentence introducing a new stage in the story. The
long periods, characteristic of Cicero's rhetoric, are
avoided. The sentences are clearly constructed, usually
of moderate length, with a series of participle phrases
leading up to the main verb. Such a style suits the
straightforward narrative such as that of the two
invasions of Britain, but there are passages in the
Commentaries where the drama of events inspires
Caesar to a more emotive style; this is illustrated by his
account of the destruction of Sabinus, as we point out in
our own commentary.

Useful books

The fullest biography of Caesar is that by M. Gelzer
(Blackwell); that of Michael Grant (Weidenfeld &
Nicolson) is also excellent. The standard book on
Caesar's Gallic campaigns is still T. Rice Holmes:
Caesar's Conquest of Gaul (Oxford). A paraphrase of
Caesar's account of the invasions of Britain, with a
useful commentary, can be found in P. Salway: *Roman
Britain*, The Oxford History of England (Oxford), ch. 2.
P. B. Ellis: *Caesar's Invasion of Britain* (Constable)
gives a good account of Celtic civilization but adds
little to Caesar's own account of the actual invasion.
Caesar: *The Gallic War*, translated by Carolyn
Hammond, World's Classics (Oxford) provides both a
good modern translation and a useful and informative
introduction.

1 The first invasion of Britain

BG 4.20–38, with omissions

   BG 4.20–22

3 hostibus nostris inde sumministrata auxilia:
although Caesar only once gives a particular instance of
help being sent from Britain (*BG* 3.9: *Veneti ... auxilia
ex Britannia, quae contra eas regiones posita est,
arcessunt*), it is probably true that this was a common
occurrence.
4–6 et si tempus ... cognovisset: Caesar here makes it
clear that this year's expedition was no more than a
reconnaissance force. The two legions he took to
Britain were the seventh and the tenth; the latter was his
crack legion, which was staunchly loyal to him.
6–7 quae omnia fere Gallis erant incognita: it is
hard to believe that the Gauls were so ignorant of
Britain in view of the close cultural and commercial
relations they had with the south of the island. The

merchants perhaps withheld information, not wanting the Romans to impinge on this market.

24 ut in ea sententia permanerent: we omit a sentence in which Caesar says that he sent Commius back with these envoys to try to win over British tribes to the Roman cause.

31–2: tenebantur quominus ... venire possent: on the use of **quominus**, see Appendix 1, p. 86.

32 has equitibus distribuit: these eighteen ships with the cavalry never reached Britain; they attempted to sail there four days after Caesar had landed in Britain but when they were already in sight of Caesar's camp, they were driven off course by a sudden storm, some back to Gaul, some to the west of Britain (see *BG* 4.26 and 28). The lack of cavalry proved a serious handicap to Caesar.

It may be thought that Caesar's preparations were inadequate. He was proposing to invade an island that, according to his own account, was completely unknown to the Roman world; he knew nothing of its geography or of the resistance he was likely to meet, and yet his only attempt to get better intelligence was to send Volusenus on a short exploration of the coast. His account of the landing suggests that he encountered far stronger resistance than he had expected. You might ask your students what they feel about this. Was this behaviour consistent with his reputation as a great general who did not risk his troops unnecessarily?

BG 4.23

You might choose to use this quickly moving chapter to illustrate Caesar's narrative method. A succession of events is presented in the simplest structural form. Ablative absolute and other participial phrases lead up to the main verbs which give the principal actions of the sentences. Events are recorded with the utmost clarity and brevity and a complete absence of rhetorical ornament; not a single word has emotional connotations. The paragraph well illustrates the remarks of Atticus in Cicero's *Brutus*, quoted in the introduction above.

BG 4.24–6

By the time Caesar had reached the beaches at Deal, the Britons were ready to oppose the landing in full force. Their military strength lay in their chariots. Caesar describes in 4.33 (omitted) the tactics employed in their use:

> Their method of fighting from chariots is as follows. First they drive around in all directions, casting missiles and generally throwing army ranks into confusion, through the panic caused by the horses and the noise of the wheels. Then, when they have wormed their way in between the cavalry squadrons, they jump down from the chariots and fight on foot. Meanwhile the charioteers gradually make their way out of the fighting, and station their chariots so that, if they are hard pressed by a host of enemies, they have a speedy retreat to their own side. Thus they provide the flexible mobility of cavalry and the stability of infantry in battle. By means of daily practice and exercises they ensure that even on the steepest of inclines they can hold their horses at full gallop, control and turn them swiftly, run along the beam and stand on the yoke – and from there get quickly back to the chariot.

In continental Gaul the chariot had been superseded by massed cavalry (Caesar enrolled Gallic cavalry in his army), so this chapter records the first occasion when the Roman legions experienced a chariot attack. It is clear that Caesar was deeply impressed by the skill and courage of the British charioteers, who were to cause him considerable difficulty during the two invasions.

48–9 praemisso equitatu et essedariis: there is little mention of ordinary cavalry elsewhere in the narrative, but Caesar used Gallic cavalry in his army and there is no reason to suppose that the British were deficient in this arm.

49–50 reliquis copiis subsecuti: 'the rest of their forces' would have been lightly armed infantry; these had no body armour and went into battle wearing no more than a pair of loose trousers; their basic weapon was the long Celtic sword. Such troops were no match for the heavily armed legionaries. The following year, when Cassivellaunus had failed to hold the line of the Thames, he dismissed all his forces except for 4,000 chariots (*BG* 5.19).

57–8 quibus rebus nostri perterriti: this is very strong language; it was unheard of for the legionaries to show fear in the face of a 'barbarian' enemy, though the Romans often represented their Gallic enemies as formidable in their sculpture (see the famous *Dying Gaul* on p. 101 of the Reader).

61ff. quod ubi Caesar animadvertit ...: Caesar saved the situation by decisive counteraction, backed by the courage of the standard-bearer of the tenth legion, the first Roman soldier, as far as we know, to land on British soil. The words of the standard bearer are given in direct speech, the first use of actual quoted words in the *Commentaries*, which marks the importance of the occasion. Such was the almost mystical significance of the legionary standard to the Roman soldier, that when the standard bearer jumped, the rest would be bound to follow. (When Augustus in 19 BC recovered from the Parthians the standards lost at Carrhae, he even issued coins with the legend *signis receptis*.)

88–9 hoc unum ... defuit: this was not the last time that lack of cavalry frustrated Caesar on this expedition.

You might ask your students to summarize the difficulties the Romans faced at the landing and the measures Caesar took to counteract these difficulties.

BG 4.27–9

We have omitted a few sentences in which Caesar describes how Commius came with the British envoys and excused his failure to return earlier on the grounds that he had been arrested by the Britons.
102 portu: this is thought to have been Ambleteuse, eight miles west of Boulogne.
108 eadem nocte accidit ut esset luna plena: spring tides, when high-water level reaches its maximum, occur at or just after the full moon, as Caesar says; on this occasion the easterly gale referred to in the previous paragraph may have driven the water even higher up than usual. The Mediterranean is virtually tideless but, as we say in the Reader, Caesar had had experience of tidal waters in the war against the Veneti the year before. His attempt to disclaim responsibility for this disaster, which might have resulted in the annihilation of his small force, seems unconvincing.

BG 4.30–32, 34

119–27 quibus rebus ... coeperunt: this chapter (4.30), consisting of one long sentence followed by a second short one, might offer a good opportunity for analysing Caesar's method in presenting complex ideas. The structure of the first sentence is: ablative absolute, followed by the subject of the sentence qualified by a relative clause; a participle agreeing with the subject is followed by a double **cum** clause, leading to the main verb (**duxerunt**); the Britons' plan is given in two short infinitive phrases preceeded by an ablative absolute; and the sentence ends with a **quod** clause giving the reasons for their decision, in which two ablative absolute phrases lead up to the conclusion **neminem ... confidebant**. Despite the length of the sentence, demanded by the complexity of the subject matter, the arrangement of the participles and the subordinate clauses, following each other in logical order, makes the meaning crystal clear. The first half leads up to **optimum factu esse duxerunt** (l. 122), the second half gives the Britons' plan, culminating in their confidence that by their action they would never suffer another Roman invasion. This complex sentence is followed by a short and simple one in which is described the action that follows their decision.
122 optimum factu: on the supine in **-u** see Appendix 1, p. 85.

128–50 at Caesar ...: these two paragraphs (4.31–2) well illustrate both Caesar's competence as a general and the determination of British resistance. 4.33 (omitted) gives Caesar's account of the British method of fighting from chariots (see above, p. 18).
136 legione ... una frumentatum missa: on the supine in **-um**, see Appendix 1, p. 85.
151 perturbatis nostris: the seventh legion was badly shaken by the attacks of the chariots

    novitate pugnae: Caesar again stresses the fearful experience of this journey into the unknown.
157 reliqui discesserunt: the disappearance of the Britons who had been coming and going from his camp warned Caesar that trouble was brewing.

BG 4.35–7

In a sentence omitted Caesar says that Commius had brought in about thirty cavalry to help. Although the Britons outnumbered the Romans greatly, they could not stand up to the heavily armed legions when they were drawn up before their camp in set formation.
169–70 tanto spatio ... quantum ... potuerunt: on comparative clauses, see Appendix 1, pp. 85–6.
176–8 ipse ... pervenerunt: Caesar's return to Gaul seems precipitate. He was afraid of bad weather at the equinox; but perhaps he had also had news that rebellion was stirring in Gaul. When he landed his troops on the mainland, a detachment marching to its camp was attacked by the Morini and had to be rescued by Caesar; following this, further operations had to be undertaken against the Morini and Menapii (4.37–8, omitted).
178–9 dierum viginti supplicatio: at the end of the campaigning season of 57 BC, when Caesar had defeated the Belgae and claimed that 'all Gaul was pacified', a *supplicatio* of fifteen days was decreed. This, he proudly says, had never been granted to anyone before (2.35). Now, after far less impressive victories, twenty days was decreed, no doubt because public opinion at Rome was deeply impressed by his venture into an unknown world overseas.

This expedition, undertaken late in the year with a small force, was no more than a large-scale reconnaissance. It had nearly come to disaster. First, the landing had been opposed with more determination than Caesar had expected. Secondly, his fleet had been destroyed by the storm coinciding with the spring tide. Thirdly, one of his two legions had been badly mauled while foraging for corn. Fourthly, a coalition of British tribes had threatened to annihilate the Roman camp. In each case Caesar had snatched victory from danger of defeat by quick reaction and fearless countermeasures. While admiring his courage and skill in adversity, we might consider that the whole expedition was rash; Caesar had underestimated the strength and determination of British resistance and had rushed into precipitate action before making adequate reconnaissance. Two factors had hampered him; first, Volusenus had failed to find a suitable harbour for the invading fleet and Caesar had had to land on an open beach; second, the cavalry had failed to arrive, perhaps through the incompetence of its commanders.

Nor had he achieved anything of importance, apart from learning that he would need a much larger force for an effective campaign. He had been in Britain for little more than a fortnight and had not penetrated more than a few miles from the Kentish coast. He still had no idea of what difficulties he might encounter if he ventured into the interior.

Questions

1 What was Caesar's motive for making this expedition and what was its purpose?
2 What mistakes did he make?
3 What evidence do you find that he was a great general?
4 How stout was the resistance of the Britons and why did they fail?
5 How well did Caesar's troops acquit themselves in these operations?
6 What was achieved by this expedition?

Illustrations

p. 58: this wall painting from the temple of Isis in Pompeii shows two Roman warships racing across the waters of a harbour. It dates from the first century AD. (National Archaeological Museum, Naples)

p. 60 (below): this model of an Iron Age chariot, which would have been drawn by two small horses, is in the National Museum of Wales.

p. 62 (above): this *denarius* of L. Hostilius Saserra dates from 48 BC. It shows a naked barbarian warrior being driven into battle on a two-horsed chariot, which may well be British. The coin was propaganda for Caesar.

(below): a skiff towing a vessel into harbour: three men row while one steers. It is a relief on a tomb in the Isola Sacra, the cemetery for Ostia, the harbour of Rome.

p. 63: a replica of a Roman eagle, one of the standards of the legions.

2 The second invasion of Britain

BG 5.8–22, with omissions

In the first seven chapters of Book 5, Caesar describes his preparations for the invasion of Britain, which he clearly intended to be his main operation the next year. On returning to Further Gaul in spring 54 BC he found that preparations were nearly complete, and he ordered the invasion fleet to assemble at Portus Itius. But before embarking he had to settle affairs in the territory of the Treveri, who were proving troublesome. He then returned to Portus Itius but the invasion again had to be postponed, since Dumnorix, the influential leader of the Aedui, was proving disloyal and refused to accompany Caesar to Britain. It was not until Dumnorix had been pursued and put to death that Caesar was free to sail, at the beginning of July, considerably later than he had intended.

BG 5.8–9

1–2 Labieno ... relicto: in leaving Labienus on the continent with only three legions and 2,000 cavalry Caesar may be thought to have taken a considerable risk. Gaul was by no means 'pacified'.

9–10 ut eam partem ... cognoverat: Caesar again landed on the open beaches near Deal. He had not learnt from the previous year's disaster and was to suffer from this mistake.

28–31 illi ... proelium committere coeperunt: it looks as if the Britons, after deciding not to oppose Caesar's landing, planned to attack him from a position of strength, in front of the river Stour, behind what they supposed to be an impregnable fortress and thick woods into which they could retire as they used the hit and run tactics for which their war chariots were so well suited. They had never experienced and were not prepared for the Romans' skill in attacking fortified positions.

BG 5.10–11

Caesar here gives the bare facts of the disaster; he makes no attempt this time to excuse what must be considered incompetence, but in compensation he lays stress on the skill, energy and efficiency by which the situation was saved.

If Caesar had reconnoitred further east, he would have found a natural harbour at Richborough protected by the isle of Thanet (this was one of the bases used in Claudius' invasion a hundred years later); this would have saved him the colossal labour of beaching his fleet and surrounding it by fortifications. The time spent on this operation (ten days) allowed the Britons to form a united army under the command of Cassivellaunus, which endangered the whole enterprise.

BG 5.11, 15, 17

65 **Cassivellauno**: we know little of Cassivellaunus except what we learn from Caesar; he was evidently trying to expand his already powerful kingdom at the expense of his neighbours, whose hostility he had incurred (see 5.20). This makes it all the more surprising that the British tribes united under his leadership.

BG 5.12–14 is an excursus on the inhabitants, resources and geography of Britain. We have omitted it because it interrupts the narrative and is largely ill-informed; some editors consider that it is an addition by another hand; if it is Caesar's work it shows how limited his knowledge of Britain was.

70ff. **equites hostium ...**: the attack made by the British cavalry and war chariots while the Romans were fortifying their camp took them by surprise; the British broke right through the Roman lines and returned without suffering any casualties. In the following chapter (5.16, omitted) Caesar describes the tactics of the British and the difficulties the Romans experienced. The heavily armed Roman legionaries could not pursue the British when they retreated and the cavalry were at risk; for the Britons often retreated on purpose, enticed them away from the legions and then jumped down from their chariots and attacked them on foot at an advantage. Caesar goes on:

> Besides, the Britons never fought in massed formation, but in scattered groups with wide spaces between them, and they had detachments arranged at intervals, which relieved each other in succession, fresh and unused troops taking the places of those who were exhausted.

The tactics used by the British were extremely effective and one detects a note of admiration in Caesar's account.

85ff. **sed meridie ...**: when the Britons attacked the foraging party, the Romans were ready for them, so that when the British broke through the cavalry screen they faced the legions drawn up for battle and had to beat a hasty retreat; the Roman cavalry, supported by the legions, pursued them so closely that they had no chance of using their usual tactics.

BG 5.18–21

100 **acutis sudibus**: Bede (AD 673–735) says in his *Ecclesiastical History* (1.2) that these stakes were still visible in his day, 'as thick as a man's thigh and covered with lead'. The remains of some stakes have been discovered at Brentford but these may have no connection with Cassivellaunus' defence of the Thames.

107ff.: Cassivellaunus after this defeat abandoned all plans to face the Romans in set battle and dismissed all his forces except for 4,000 charioteers. He now adopted guerilla tactics, continually harrying the Roman advance and depriving them of all food supplies on their route. Caesar makes it clear that this made things very difficult for the Romans. If the Trinobantes (see n. on l. 120 below) had not come to the rescue and supplied corn, Caesar might have been unable to continue his advance.

117–18 **tantum ... quantum**: on comparative clauses, see Appendix 1, pp. 85–6.

120 **Trinobantes**: in a passage from 5.20 that we have omitted, Caesar tells us that the king of the Trinobantes had been killed by Cassivellaunus and that his son Mandracius had come to Gaul to seek Caesar's protection. Now they asked Caesar to send him back to them and protect him from Cassivellaunus. After Caesar had left Britain the Catuvellauni continued their expansion and the evidence of coins shows that by about 15 BC they had assimilated the territory of the Trinobantes.

127 **oppidum Cassivellauni**: although Cassivellaunus' fortress at Wheathampstead must have looked formidable, it proved no serious obstacle to the Romans with their long experience of attacking fortified positions. Wheathampstead was excavated by Sir Mortimer Wheeler in 1932; its identification with Cassivellaunus' stronghold is not universally accepted but it seems extremely probable.

BG 5.22

Cassivellaunus' last fling was to order a surprise attack on the naval camp, a good strategic move which threatened Caesar's rear, and, as we learn from a letter written by Caesar to Cicero on 5 August, Caesar hastened back there to see that all was well.

141–2 **legatos [per Atrebatem Commium, omitted] de deditione ad Caesarem mittit**: Cassivellaunus had fought a skilful campaign with considerable success but was now ready to come to terms. How were the negotiations made through Commius, who was with Caesar's army? It has been suggested that Caesar, satisfied with what he had achieved and anxious to get back to Gaul where revolt was imminent, sent him to Cassivellaunus to open negotiations. The terms agreed were not harsh; Cassivellaunus remained king of the Catuvellauni and was succeeded by his son; he probably had no intention of paying tribute if Caesar was tied down in Gaul. Caesar had achieved nothing of permanent significance, as Tacitus remarks (see Reader, p. 80), nor did the Romans acquire any booty from the expedition, as Cicero told Atticus (*ad Att.* 4.18.5):

> a Quinto fratre et a Caesare accepi a.d. viii Kal.
> Nov. litteras datas a litoribus Britanniae proximae
> a.d. vi Kal.Oct. confecta Britannia, obsidibus
> acceptis, nulla praeda, imperata tamen pecunia,
> exercitum e Britannia reportabant.

> I received on 24 October letters from my brother
> Quintus and Caesar dated 25 September from the
> shores of nearer Britain; they had settled Britain,
> received hostages, no booty but tribute was
> imposed; they were bringing back the army from
> Britain.

Questions

1 What mistakes did Caesar make on this expedition?
2 How successful were the tactics employed by
Cassivellaunus in his defensive campaign?
3 What do you feel is Caesar's estimate of the Britons'
performance in these operations?
4 What had Caesar achieved by his invasion of Britain?

Illustrations

p. 70: the view is over the river Stour to the hill where
the Britons had their fort. Some of the great ditch-works
can still be seen on the hill (not visible in the
photograph).
p. 72: this *testudo* is a relief from the Column of Marcus
Aurelius, erected in imitation of Trajan's Column. It
celebrated Marcus Aurelius' victories over the Germans
and Sarmatians (AD 169–76). The sculpting is generally
considered to be inferior to that on Trajan's Column.
p. 78 (above): the coin of the Catuvellauni portrays
their king Tasciovanus (a later king than
Cassivellaunus). It was minted in Camolodunum
between 20 BC and AD 10.
   (below): the upper portion of a reclining figure in
Italian marble, probably mid-second century AD. This
may be a personification both of the river Thames and
of the river Styx, which separated the living from the
dead. (London Museum)
p. 81: this coin of AD 46–7 shows a triumphal arch with
the inscription *de Britann[ia]* ('concerning Britain'). On
top of the arch is an equestrian statue, presumably of
the emperor, between two trophies. Minted at Rome, the
coin dates from the reign of Claudius, in which Britain
was more effectively conquered than it had been by
Caesar.

3 Revolt in Gaul 1: The ambush of Sabinus and Cotta

BG 5.26–37, with omissions

Caesar's legions were distributed as follows (*BG* 5.24,
see map, p. 57): he himself was at Samarobriva
(Amiens); one, commanded by C. Fabius, was stationed
amongst the Morini, a second under Quintus Cicero
(Cicero's brother) amongst the Nervii, possibly at
Binche, about 75 miles east of Amiens; a third amongst
the Esubii; a fourth under Labienus on the borders of
the Treveri, perhaps at Mouzon on the Meuse; three
amongst the Belgae; one, commanded by Crassus (son
of the triumvir), amongst the Bellovaci, 25 miles west
of Amiens; and one and a half amongst the Eburones
under Sabinus and Cotta at Aduatica (near Tongres?),
about 50 miles north-east of Binches (see 6.32). The
exact positions of the legions' winter quarters are not
known, except for those of Caesar.

   It is worth remarking that whereas Caesar's account
of the invasions of Britain is first-hand, since he was
present at all the actions he describes, his account of the
attack on Sabinus' camp and the subsequent disaster
must have been pieced together from the reports of the
few survivors. It is remarkably detailed and some must
be his own reconstruction of events, e.g. Ambiorix's
speech in 5.27 and the description of the council of war
in 5.28–30. The survivors could scarcely have
remembered the actual words of Cotta and Sabinus
which are so dramatically reported by Caesar.

   We know that Caesar was so devastated by the loss
of a legion and a half that he let his beard grow until he
had avenged it; his anger and grief is reflected in the
emotive way in which he describes the events. You
might illustrate this from 5.30, where Sabinus' words
are recorded in direct speech (the only other
occurrences of direct speech in our extracts are the
words of the standard-bearer of the tenth legion when
he leaps from his ship (4.25), and the challenge of Pullo
to Vorenus (5.44); all three are very dramatic moments.)
It is hardly too much to say that he has here constructed
a drama, based on known facts but informed by his own
evaluation of events, that is by his admiration for
Cotta's behaviour and his contempt for Sabinus'.

BG 5.26–7

3 **Sabino**: Sabinus' full name was Q. Titurius Sabinus
and Caesar refers to him sometimes as Titurius,
sometimes as Sabinus; to avoid confusion we have
always called him Sabinus. He had served as legate
throughout Caesar's campaigns in Gaul and had won a
victory over the Veneti.

6 oppugnatum: on the supine expressing purpose, see Appendix 1, p. 85.

14–15 pro Caesaris in se beneficiis: Ambiorix was subject to a tribute imposed by the neighbouring Aduatici when Caesar conquered the latter in 57 BC; Caesar freed him from this tribute and released his son and nephew whom he had captured; by conferring these benefits he no doubt hoped to have in him a firm supporter in this region.

19 coactu civitatis: kingship was elective amongst the Celtic tribes and the kings were subject to public opinion (compare the excuses offered by the British chieftains in 4.27).

25 priusquam finitimi sentiant: i.e. before the neighbouring Gallic tribes knew of their move.

26–7 alter milia passuum quinquaginta: if the sites of the camps have been correctly identified, Cicero's camp was nearer to 70 miles away. By forced marches this distance might be covered in two days.

BG 5.28–30

46–53: Sabinus' speech, most of which we have omitted, is constructed as a carefully balanced piece which suggests a rhetorical exercise rather than an off-the-cuff argument made in a council of war. We hope that we have included enough of it to suggest this.

48–9 neque is sum ... qui ... terrear: 'I am not the sort of man to be terrified'. The subjunctive in the relative clause is 'generic': see Appendix 1, p. 86. Sabinus' arguments up to this point have been reasoned; he now makes an emotional appeal which is intended to be heard by the soldiers. He uses devices of rhetoric, not often found in Caesar: **reiecti et relegati** (doublet with assonance), **aut ferro aut fame** (doublet with alliteration).

BG 5.31

58–9 sic ... ut quibus esset persuasum: 'they so set out as men who had been persuaded'; the **ut** clause is not consecutive but comparative; the subjunctive used in the relative clause is probably generic = 'like the sort of men ...'. Caesar is here not giving facts but making a comment to show the folly of Sabinus' plan.

BG 5.32–7

69–72 tum demum Sabinus ... at Cotta: as disaster strikes, Caesar condemns Sabinus' behaviour and praises that of Cotta without qualification.

69 qui nihil ante providisset: the relative with the subjunctive expresses cause (see Appendix 1, p. 86); so also **Cotta, qui cogitasset ... non fuisset** (ll. 73–4).

69–70 trepidare et concursare: on historic infinitives, see Appendix 1, p. 85.

78 iusserunt pronuntiare: 'ordered (officers) to proclaim ...'. We prefer to say 'ordered it to be proclaimed', and Caesar himself sometimes uses this impersonal construction, e.g. **Ambiorix pronuntiari iubet** (l. 87).

83–5 tametsi ... ponebant: as he praises the conduct of the soldiers, who were not to blame for the disaster, his language again becomes emotive. Cf. **nihil quod ipsis esset indignum committebant** (ll. 91–2).

96 rogatum: on the supine expressing purpose, see Appendix 1, p. 85.

In 5.36–7 Caesar condemns both the cowardice and the folly of Sabinus, contrasting it with the courage of Cotta. One might take a different view of the events; if the situation was militarily hopeless, was it not prudent and responsible for the commanding officer to attempt to negotiate a surrender to try to save his troops from certain death? But both Caesar and Cotta knew that a Roman should never negotiate with an armed enemy and that to negotiate with Gauls was the height of folly.

Questions

1 What were the arguments for and against the Romans leaving their camp and attempting to reach another legion?

2 How does Caesar condemn the conduct of Sabinus? How does he praise that of Cotta and the soldiers? Do you consider that Sabinus deserved to be so roundly condemned?

3 What evidence do you find that Caesar's account was influenced by the anger and grief he felt at this disaster?

4 Cotta implies (ll. 100–101) that a Roman should never negotiate with an armed enemy; does this principle seem sound to you?

Illustrations

p. 88: this frieze from Trajan's Column shows soldiers building a fort. 'The buildings are rendered in a conventional way. They are obviously out of scale with the people. The battlements round the walls do not look nearly high enough for a soldier patrolling the ramparts to hide behind them, and the walls look as though they are made of masonry, whereas they were made of turves, each turf cut to standard army specifications, $1\frac{1}{2}$ Roman feet by 1 by half a foot thick. The two vertical faces of the wall were made of turf, and the filling between them was earth and rubble from the ditch outside the wall. A turf and a basket of rubble are being

passed up to the right of centre in this picture'
(R. L. Dalladay). The wood to the left will form the
basis for the sentry walk and fighting platform inside
the battlements.
p. 89: from Trajan's Column: the soldiers on the right
are felling trees while one on the left fetches water.
Also on the left, Trajan points to a fort deserted by the
enemy.

4 Revolt in Gaul 2: The siege of Cicero's camp

BG 5.38–52, with omissions

Although Caesar was not present at the attack on
Cicero's camp, he would have received a full and
detailed report from Cicero himself and his officers.
The story moves fast, event succeeding event with just
enough detail to add to the excitement (e.g. Cicero
being restrained by the soldiers from working himself to
death).

BG 5.40–43

43–4 se adiutore utantur ... mittant: subjunctives of
indirect command. Despite his desperate predicament,
Cicero answers as though the Gauls would soon be
begging Caesar for clemency. Compare Cicero's
haughty answer to the Gauls with the reaction of
Sabinus (5.28–9).
45–6 vallo ... cingunt: after failing to take the camp by
assault, the Gauls attempt circumvallation (just as
Caesar did later at Alesia); their siege tactics had been
learnt from Roman captives. To carry out this operation
would have required tremendous manpower; in 5.49,
Caesar says that the Gallic forces which marched to
meet him numbered 60,000.

BG 5.44

The vivid description of the exploit of Pullo and
Vorenus must have been reported to Caesar by
spectators. His admiration for their courage is typical of
Caesar who several times commends individual acts of
bravery (e.g. the standard bearer of the tenth legion,
who led the landing in the first invasion of Britain,
4.25). In recounting this incident in detail Caesar uses
quoted words, which, as we have seen, he does rarely
and only for dramatic effect.
      You might ask your students what they feel about
the exploit of Pullo and Vorenus. Do they admire their
brilliant courage, as Caesar does, or consider that they
were recklessly irresponsible?

BG 5.45–6

To save Cicero, Caesar not only had to act quickly but
also had to take a calculated risk. He had to leave
Samarobriva adequately garrisoned (see 5.47).
Labienus could not leave his camp because of the threat
from the Treveri. Fabius, stationed amongst the Morini,
carried out his orders to meet Caesar *en route* for
Cicero's camp. The other legions were stationed too far
off to bring help in time. He therefore decided to march
against a Gallic horde of unknown size (they proved to
number about 60,000) with a force of two legions well
under strength (about 7,000 men). The whole operation
was carried out with a speed, determination and
courage which are a supreme example of Caesar's
generalship.
92 quanto ... gravior atque asperior ... tanto ...: on
comparative clauses see Appendix 1, pp. 85–6.

BG 5.49–52

Caesar's tactics in deceiving the Gauls into believing
that his forces were even smaller than they were and
convincing them that the Romans were in a panic were
masterly. Even though the sudden sally took the enemy
completely by surprise, it is remarkable that with 400
cavalry and about 7,000 infantry he could route a force
of about 60,000 men.
184–5 Ciceronem ... legionemque collaudat: it was
characteristic of Caesar to give praise where praise was
due, just as he condemned cowardice and failure
unequivocally. He not only praised Cicero and the
legion as a whole but gave individual recognition to all
who had distinguished themselves. He followed this up
by a speech to comfort his troops and raise their morale.
This way he secured the intense loyalty of his troops,
who were ready to fight to the death for him even in
civil war.

Questions

1 Compare the behaviour of Cicero with that of
Sabinus in a similar crisis.
2 What qualities of generalship did Caesar show in this
crisis?
3 What qualities did (a) the Romans (b) the Gauls show
in this operation?

Illustrations

p. 97: this Roman bronze of a splendidly dressed Gallic
prisoner dates from the imperial period. (British
Museum, London)
p. 98: this relief is from the Arch of Constantine (AD
315) which was made up of fragments from older

monuments. Gibbon described it as 'a melancholy proof of the decline of the arts, and a singular testimony of the meanest vanity'. However, situated next to the towering ruin of the Colosseum, it makes a powerful impression. The soldier in the right foreground is full of suppressed energy and enthusiasm, and the banners fly in the wind. The general is probably Hadrian.

p. 99: from Trajan's Column: auxiliary soldiers defend the fort from Dacian attack. The Dacian figures are portrayed in a heroic light.

p. 101: this poignant statue, representing a Celtic warrior who lies mortally wounded on the ground awaiting death, is a Roman copy of one of the statues dedicated by Attalus I at Pergamon. It is known as the *Dying Gaul*. (Capitoline Museum, Rome)

Catullus

Catullus the poet

Of all ancient writers Catullus is the most sympathetic to young readers and in our selection we have chosen poems which we consider most likely to evoke a personal response from students. We have limited ourselves to shorter poems, most of which can, we hope, be assimilated at one go. Important aspects of Catullus' art are therefore not illustrated; there is little evidence here, at least superficially, that he was *doctus*, and we have not used poems which would necessitate an explanation of his Alexandrianism.

It is scarcely possible to give here a full critical introduction to Catullus but it is worth stressing his originality. The group of poets to which he belonged, the *poetae novi*, as the poetically conservative Cicero contemptuously called them, consciously broke with the old traditions of Roman poetry, which since its beginnings (Livius Andronicus, fl. 240 BC) had been limited to what might be called 'public poetry' – epic and drama, ultimately based on classical Greek models. The Neoterics (the Greek word *neoteroi* = 'newer'), the name given to Catullus' group, drew their literary inspiration from the poets who flourished in Alexandria about 250 BC, above all from Callimachus, to whom Catullus implicitly acknowledges his debt in several poems.

Callimachus rejected epic as a viable genre. He says that his poetry will be small scale, light and original:

> Others may bray like the long-eared ass,
> But may I be the miniature, the winged poet.

This extract is from the Prologue to the *Aitia*, in which he lays down his literary principles; the passage is paraphrased by Virgil (*Eclogues* 6.1–5), echoed by Horace (*Odes* 1.6.5–10) and acknowledged by Propertius (3.1.1ff.). The Augustan poets were all, in a sense, Neoterics; there was no going back from the achievement of Catullus.

Catullus' originality has several facets. First in his choice of subject matter: he uses poetry as a vehicle for expressing his feelings on any topic which comes to mind, from the trivial to the profound. No Roman poet had done this before; indeed, before Catullus personal feelings had hardly been the subject matter of Latin poetry at all. Secondly, he was the first to use the metres of Greek lyric poetry (a fact which Horace chooses to ignore), and he develops the elegiac couplet, only used in Latin for epigrams until his time, in longer poems and so becomes the founder of Latin elegiac love poetry. Thirdly, his diction is strikingly different from that of his predecessors; he could handle the high poetic style if he wished to (e.g. in the 'Peleus and Thetis', poem 64), but in the shorter poems he often uses colloquial diction with superb effect.

The world of Catullus

Just as Catullus and his fellow poets belong to a recognizable poetic group, so do he and his friends form a clearly defined social group. The two groups are in fact impossible to separate, and the characteristics of Catullus' circle of friends are made clear in the language of his poems.

Charm and social poise are of paramount importance: *lepidus* (charming, delightful) and related words appear twelve times in the poems, *venustus* (charming, pretty) words eleven. Wit is an essential quality: *sal* (salt, i.e. flavoursome humour) words occur nine times, *facetus* (clever, humorous) words six. Learning is important too: *doctus* (learned) comes four times; and so is novelty (1.1). Useful adjuncts are elegance and good looks: *bellus* (pretty, handsome) scores a count of fifteen. Also notching up fifteen is *beatus* (happy, fortunate) with its suggestion of the blissful world to which the poet and his friends have gained admission. And you do not have to be a person to qualify for the Catullan set: Sirmio, the peninsula which is his home, is called *venusta* (3.12). The bonds of affectionate intimacy, sometimes mocking, sometimes sympathetic, which hold this world together are suggested by the constant use of diminutives, many of them coined by the poet.

A number of Catullus' poems describe people whose attributes disqualify them from admission to his charmed circle. Their words are *illepidus*, *invenustus*, *insulsus*, *infacetus* (negatives of the Latin words in the last paragraph), *ineptus* (gauche) and *turpis* (ugly, repulsive). Some of them are bad writers. What all of them lack is *urbanitas*, the social grace and playful behaviour associated with the city which distinguish Catullus' set from the boors and the country bumpkins.

These outsiders are the victims of his withering scorn. Such violations of the Catullan code as vulgarity and insensitivity can be punished by vicious crudity. Brutal coarseness is presumably the only way to get through to such boors. Thus a thuggish and obscene voice is heard alongside the playful and learned wit and the passionate intensity for which the poet is famous.

Catullus' set is held together by bonds of love and friendship – two concepts which the poet considers one and which he takes very seriously indeed: *amo, amicus* and related worlds occur 110 times. Treachery from lover and friend alike evokes savage outbursts. Catullus repeatedly asserts his belief in *pietas*, the concept that binds society together.

The primacy of friendship and its bonds (*fides*) is in fact the main and unifying feature of Catullus' poetry. For the poet's tragedy in his affair with Lesbia is that he is demanding far too much of it. He longs for an idealized friendship as well as a sexual relationship. This comes across most startlingly in 72.3–4:

> dilexi tum te non tantum ut vulgus amicam,
> sed pater ut gnatos diligit et generos.

> I loved you then not only as an ordinary man loves his girlfriend but as a father loves his sons and sons-in-law.

To us the stressing of a father's love for his sons-in-law as well as his sons may appear somewhat absurd. But surely Catullus wishes to evoke a particularly altruistic and non-physical form of love. In addition, by the emphasis on family ties, he links love with *pietas*. In one of the last poems of the collection (109.5–6) he expresses the hope that he and his girl may be able to keep a treaty of sacred friendship, *hoc sanctae foedus amicitiae*. It is a telling phrase, close to the heart of the deep emotion which informs Catullus' poetry.

Treatment of the poems in class

We have said that the short poems of Catullus are more likely to evoke a personal response from young readers than anything else in ancient literature. How are they to be treated in class? One axiom is that the teacher must not attempt to tell his class *ex cathedra* how they should respond to a poem; rather the class should feel its way to a response through a process of question and answer.

The first task is to establish the sense of the poem. Here it is best for the teacher to begin by reading the whole poem, or if it is too long, its first half, aloud in

Latin. To do this successfully the teacher must be thoroughly at home with the metres of Catullus. (In Appendix 2 of the Reader, we explain the metres of all the poems in our selection.) In this reading the rhythms of the poem must come across clearly. Then the sense must be established either by translation or by asking comprehension questions. If translation is preferred, it often pays to allow any member of the class to chip in (the so-called 'mosaic method' of translation), rather than putting on one individual. If comprehension questions are used, the teacher must be at pains to ensure that the Latin is fully understood at sense level. When this has been done, the poem should be read aloud in Latin again before discussion begins.

Teachers will not at this level be attempting to give or to elicit a critical exegesis; the terms of criticism need not be used. Our aim is to help pupils respond by ascertaining that they understand what the poet is saying and what emotions he intends to convey. For instance in poem 31 (p. 132, *Paene insularum*), the key question may be 'Why is the poet so happy?' or 'What does the poet feel on returning home?' Other questions might be 'What is he glad to be rid of?' and 'What does he particularly like about coming home?' Always ask pupils for references to the Latin to support the views they offer.

Simple questions on structure are often helpful, e.g. 'How does the poem begin?' (by greeting Sirmio, ll. 1–3); 'How does it end?' (by greeting Sirmio again – *salve* – and by telling it to laugh for joy). Questions on imagery are often appropriate, e.g. *solutis curis*: the cares are like a heavy pack which the mind unties.

At the end of such discussion one might hope that the class would not only have formed a personal response but would have begun to see how the poet achieves his purpose. Catullus' poems are not the spontaneous overflow of powerful feeling which they often appear but the expression of emotion under conscious intellectual control.

Practical criticism of the sort suggested above is time-consuming and we do not suppose that you will be able to treat every poem in this way. But if you are successful with some of the poems, this will influence the whole attitude of your pupils to their reading of ancient (and modern) poetry.

These books are worth consulting:

K. Quinn, ed.: *Catullus: The Poems*, Macmillan (the most convenient modern edition)

The Poems of Catullus, ed. with introduction, translation and brief notes by Guy Lee (World's Classics series), Oxford (text with good translation on facing page)

W. V. Clausen, 'The New Direction in Poetry', in *The Cambridge History of Classical Literature*, vol. 2,

ed. E. J. Kenney and W. V. Clausen, Cambridge,
pp. 178–206

J. Ferguson: *Catullus* (Greece & Rome New Surveys in
the Classics), Oxford

R. O. A. M. Lyne: *The Latin Love Poets: From Catullus
to Horace*, Oxford, pp. 19–61

K. Quinn, ed.: *Approaches to Catullus*, Cambridge

T. P. Wiseman: *Catullus and his World*, Cambridge

Introduction

p. 102, l. 2: Verona was no more than a hill fort before
the invasion of the Cimbri (102 BC); after their defeat
Transpadane Gaul was settled by Roman colonists,
amongst whom may have been Catullus' father or
grandfather. Verona rapidly became prosperous and
Catullus' father must have been one of its leading
citizens, seeing that Julius Caesar was a friend of the
family and remained so even after Catullus had attacked
him in several obscene poems.

p. 102, ll. 3–4: the dates of Catullus' life are in fact
uncertain, but those we give are not unlikely.

p. 103, l. 9: 'one slim volume': it is possible that, like
the history of Cornelius (poem 1), Catullus' poetry was
published in three books.

Poem 1

In this dedicatory poem, Catullus establishes his artistic
claims at the outset: his poetry has novelty and charm
(l. 1). While self-deprecatory in his affectation of
modesty (**libellum** (l. 1), **nugas** (l. 4), ll. 8–9), he has
worked hard at his poetry (l. 2 – see n.) and hopes that it
will last (l. 10).

2 **arida ... expolitum**: Roman books consisted of a roll
of papyrus with the text laid out in a series of columns.
The reader unrolled this with the right hand and rolled it
up again with the left. The word **modo** suggests that the
dedicatee is receiving a book which is, as we would say,
hot off the press. As well as the literal meaning,
Catullus stresses the considerable labour that has gone
into the writing of his little book.

3ff. **Corneli ...**: the dedicatee is Cornelius Nepos (c.
110–24 BC), a contemporary of Catullus from the same
part of Italy. The work referred to is his *Chronica*, now
lost, an epitome of the history of the world in three
volumes, perhaps like Catullus' own poetry. As well as
history, Cornelius wrote biography, moralizing essays
and erotic poetry.

1 Catullus and his friends

Poems 50, 53, 49, 93, 14, 9, 13

Poem 50

A letter in verse, a favourite form for Catullus, in four
sentences; the first (ll. 1–6) gives the reader the
information he needs to know; the second (ll. 7–13)
describes the feelings the day excited in Catullus; the
third (ll. 14–17) explains the reasons for writing the
poem; the last (ll. 18–21, actually two sentences)
requests another meeting.

1 **Licini**: Gaius Licinius Calvus (82–c. 47 BC) was, as
we can tell from the extremely scanty fragments of his
poems that survive, a poet of similar range of subjects
(including attacks on Caesar) to Catullus.

2 **lusimus**: this means **1** we enjoyed ourselves; **2** we
wrote amusing verse (cf. Ovid, who describes himself
as *tenerorum lusor amorum*, *Tristia* 4.10.1).

tabellis: wooden tablets coated with wax; the wax,
once written on, could be smoothed out and the writing
process started up again, ideally suited for Catullus' and
Calvus' needs.

3 **delicatos**: the basic meaning is 'delightful',
'charming'. Overtones are: **1** 'sophisticated', 'precious',
'smart', almost 'decadent'; **2** something like 'risqué'
(Quinn).

7–13 **atque illinc ...**: see question 4. In humorous
hyperbole, Catullus uses the standard imagery and
language of love poetry to convey the intensity of his
poetical feelings: 'he is on fire (*incensus*); his thoughts
are deranged (*furore*); he is to be pitied (*miserum*); he is
off his food, he cannot sleep; he wants only to be with
Calvus again. Cf. Dido in the opening lines of *Aeneid* 4
[see p. 148]' (Quinn). Your pupils may come to the
conclusion that Calvus is gay, though the more
discerning will see that Catullus is in fact parodying
love poetry: the symptoms of unrequited love are piled
up rather too thickly and lead to the mock-solemnity of
the final warning.

18 **cave**: scanned **căvĕ**. Catullus is warning Calvus not
to reject his request for a second meeting; the language
of love is continued.

Poem 53

Publius Vatinius was the tribune who in the year of
Caesar's consulship put through the *concilium plebis* the
legislation that Caesar wanted. As a henchman of
Caesar he became extremely unpopular and was
attacked by Cicero in 56 BC. But Cicero was compelled
by the triumvirs to defend him on a bribery charge in
54; this was probably the occasion of the poem, when

Calvus (see n. on 50.1 above) was prosecuting Vatinius for the second time. The anecdote *num, si iste est disertus ...* is told by the elder Seneca (*Cont.* 7.4.6).
5 **di magni ...**: the point of the epigram lies in the last line, in which unfortunately the key word **salaputium** is obscure. Bickel's suggestion that it means **mentula salax** ('lecherous cock') may be on the right lines.

Poem 49

At first glance, this is an effusive letter of thanks to Cicero for some service he had done him. Quinn suggests that it may be ironical: the language of the first four lines may be felt to go over the top and, as Quinn says, Catullus certainly did not believe that he was the worst of poets. (See question.) Catullus returned from Bithynia at about the time of Cicero's defence of Caelius Rufus (April 56 BC) (on this case, see pp. 124–7 of the Reader). If this was the Caelius who stole Clodia from Catullus and if the occasion of the poem was Cicero's successful defence of Caelius in a prosecution initiated by Clodia, the poem may indeed be ironical; and as Cicero destroyed Clodia's character in his speech, there may also be a note of bitter exultation underlying the extravagant language.

Poem 93

Catullus attacks Caesar in three other poems (29, 54, 57) which are all obscenely abusive; according to Suetonius (*Div. Iul.* 73) the two men were later reconciled. Caesar invited Catullus to dinner and continued to enjoy the hospitality of Catullus' father.

Poem 14

Another letter in verse, in which Catullus pretends furious indignation at the gift Calvus (see n. on 50.1 above) has sent him on the eve of the Saturnalia, an anthology of bad poetry. The poem is also an oblique attack on the sort of poetry which Catullus and his circle despised – epic in the old Roman tradition (compare his attack on the *Annals* of Volusius in poem 36: *annales Volusi, cacata carta*, etc.)
The poet plunges straight into his indignation at Calvus' gift (ll. 1–3), then asks why his friend should have done such a thing (ll. 4–11); a further outburst of indignation (ll. 12–16) is followed by a threat to pay him back in kind (ll. 17–20), and the poem ends by sending the **pessimi poetae** packing.
9 **Sulla**: perhaps Cornelius Epicadus, a freedman of the dictator Sulla.
14 **continuo**: best taken as an adverb = 'straight away', 'on the spot'; but it could agree with **die** = 'all day long'

(a lingering death from boredom).
20 **his suppliciis**: 'with this torture', i.e. boredom.

Question 1: opinions divide on this matter, but Catullus certainly writes as if he thought it was a joke (**salse**, l. 16) and we know that Calvus shared Catullus' poetic tastes.

Poem 9

Veranius had been in Spain with Fabullus, to whom the next poem in our selection is written. They had sent Catullus a present of Spanish napkins (see poem 12). The poem reads like an unpremeditated outburst of joy but it is carefully constructed, so that the reader knows enough about the situation to share Catullus' feelings. 'A good example of lyric form under conscious control' (Quinn).

Poem 13

A letter addressed to Fabullus inviting him to dinner, perhaps on his return from Spain. The poem looks like a parody of the invitation poem: Philodemus of Gadara, a contemporary of Catullus, wrote an elegiac epigram inviting his patron to dinner, saying that the food and wine won't be up to much but that conversation will be good (*Anth. Pal.* 11.44). Later Horace writes to invite Maecenas to dinner but warns him that he cannot expect the best wines (*Odes* 1.20). Catullus goes one better (or worse); instead of a poor dinner, the guest will get no dinner at all unless he brings it with him.
4 **candida**: a pale skin was considered a sign of beauty.
11–12 **nam unguentum dabo ...**: Quinn suggests that the party will be a foursome and that the scent will not be that which any Roman host would provide for his guests, but the aura which emanated from his mistress. Compare Virgil: *Aeneid* 1.402–4, where Venus is described as she leaves Aeneas: *ambrosiaeque comae divinum vertice odorem/spiravere* ('and her ambrosial locks breathed out a heavenly perfume from her head'). This interpretation certainly gives real wit and point to the line.
14 **totum ... nasum**: Fabullus will wish that all his senses can be concentrated in one, his sense of smell.

Illustrations

p. 104: see note on cover illustration, p. 5 above.
p. 107: the curia stands behind the columns of the temple of Castor. To the left is the triple Arch of Septimius Severus (AD 203).
p. 108: this relief from Veii in Etruria dating from the second century AD shows a bearded teacher looking

down at his pupil who is reading from an open scroll. (Harrow School)

p. 110: this red-figure *kylix* (drinking cup) made in Athens c. 490–480 BC shows a drinking party. A youth and a bearded man recline on two couches. With them are women entertainers. A youth enters from the left holding a musical instrument. (British Museum, London)

p. 111: this swag of leaves, fruits and nuts decorates a cinerary urn used to bury a child. Made from Carrara marble, it dates from about 120–140 BC. Compare this with the frontispiece of the Reader. (British Museum, London)

p. 112: a Roman scent bottle of gold-banded glass, dating from the first century AD. (British Museum, London)

2 Catullus in love

Poems 51, 2, 3, 5, 43, 109, 70, 72, 85, 8, 76, 77, Cicero: *pro Caelio* 49–50

p. 114, l. 17: the identification of Catullus' Lesbia with Clodia, the sister of Publius Clodius, is made by Apuleius (fl. AD 150) as if it were uncontroversial and it has been accepted by most scholars since. Clodius had two sisters and we assume that Lesbia is the notorious Clodia, wife of Metellus Celer; but some modern scholars, e.g. Wiseman, consider that she was more probably his other sister. It is common practice to treat the Lesbia poems as if they were autobiographical but this is by no means certain. Our arrangement of the poems in a biographical sequence seems to us at least a plausible reconstruction and it would be a very austere teacher who would reject such a gambit in introducing Catullus' poetry to young pupils.

Poem 51

Sappho, the Greek poetess from whom Catullus here translates, was born in Lesbos in the late seventh century BC. L. P. Wilkinson's influential view that it was this poem which launched the love affair between Catullus and Clodia may be right. It can equally well be seen, however, as a statement of the paralysing effect the presence of the loved one has on the poet and in that case could be the product of any stage of their relationship.

2 **si fas est**: it might be tempting divine providence to suggest that any human could be superior to the gods.

The poem may end with a stanza here omitted which reads:

otium, Catulle, tibi molestum est.
otio exsultas nimiumque gestis.
otium et reges prius et beatas
  perdidit urbes.

It's the fact that you have nothing to do, Catullus, that's your trouble: you take far too much restless and riotous pleasure in that: yet it's that which has before now ruined kings and prosperous cities.

If this stanza belongs to poem 51, the point will be that Catullus' idleness is what lays him open to this paralysis in his emotional life.

Poem 2

Though the poet gives no name to his girl, this is generally taken as one of the Lesbia poems. It is a parody of a prayer, in which not a god but a pet bird is addressed. Meleager had written prayers to a locust and to a cicada (*Anth. Pal.* 7.195 and 6), but this is the first time in existing classical literature that a sparrow is invoked.

Why a sparrow, not the most obvious of pets? Sappho (1.9–10) represents Aphrodite, the goddess of love, as riding in a chariot drawn by sparrows, and sparrows were emblematic of lechery and salaciousness in the ancient world. There is also the theory, which goes back at least as far as the Renaissance humanist Poliziano in his *Miscellanea* of 1485, that the Latin word for sparrow, *passer*, refers to the poet's phallus (see R. W. Hopper: 'In Defence of Catullus' Dirty Sparrow', *Greece and Rome*, vol. 32, pp. 162–75).

The poem is written in one long sentence; **passer** is vocative and the following seven lines all qualify this vocative. With the main clause beginning at l. 9, the focus of attention shifts from the sparrow and its mistress to the poet. He cannot play with the sparrow (the bird of Venus) and cannot relieve the sad cares (**curae** = the cares of love) of his heart.

5 **nitenti**: Wiseman (pp. 137ff.) takes **nitenti** as agreeing with **meae puellae** (supplied) and **desiderio meo** as ablative – 'shining (i.e. her eyes bright) with longing for me'. Her pain is caused by her longing for Catullus; or is it? **credo**, as Wiseman says, is thus the crucial word. Neither lover has yet declared his/her love.

Poem 3

The *Greek Anthology* contains a number of poems about the death of animals (7.189–216). But the control of tone exercised by Catullus in this dirge is unrivalled. His poem maintains its unity of feeling, while shifting its tone abruptly from one stage to another: an invitation to mourn (ll. 1–2); a statement of the cause of mourning (ll. 3–5); a summary of the qualities and achievements of the dead bird (ll. 6–10) who is now hopping along on his last journey (ll. 11–12); an indignant outburst against death (ll. 13–16); a final glimpse of the mourning girl (ll. 17–18).

The plural **Veneres Cupidinesque** (l. 1 – cf. 13.2), by setting us in the world of Hellenistic *putti*, undermines excessive seriousness. **Veneres** leads straight on to a key word of the Catullan set, **venustus** (l. 2; cf. **bellus** (ll. 14 and 15) and the affectionate diminutives of ll. 16 and 18). There is constant tension in the poem between the earnest concept of mourning and the colloquialism of the language (**venustus**, l. 2, **mellitus**, l. 6, **modo huc modo illuc**, l. 9, **male**, ll. 13 and 16, **bellus**, ll. 14 and 15). The simplicity of diction is especially effective in the hopping alliteration of l. 11 (**qui nunc it per iter**), which is then followed by a line of the most impressive solemnity. The sparrow, the most diminutive of birds, is acting on a stage which is too grand for it, just as the curse on Orcus, the king of the underworld (ll. 13–14), is out of all proportion to the situation.

If the **passer** is Catullus' phallus, the poem becomes on one level a lament over impotence (see notes on poem 2 and Hopper, pp. 165ff.)

14–15: the elisions of **ae** in **quae** and **em** in **passerem** 'help to convey the devouring power of death' (Ferguson).

17–18 **meae puellae**: the sudden switch to **mea puella** in the last two lines makes explicit what was suggested by the first line – that this is a love poem rather than a dirge.

Poem 5

1 **vivamus ... amemus**: 'we' conveys 'together' – 'we two against the world' (Wiseman), unmoved by the disapproval that their illicit love provokes in their puritanical elders.

The impact of this poem seems to come partly from the positioning of the words: **vivamus ... amemus** – first and last words in an end-stopped line; **soles ... nobis** emphatically placed at the beginning of consecutive lines; **lux**, a striking monosyllabic line ending, juxtaposed to **nox** at the start of the next line; the successive lines beginning **dein ... deinde ... dein ...**

The directness and economy of Catullus makes both translations look pretty poor stuff. The comparison of translations is a stimulating but time-consuming exercise, which leads pupils unawares towards an understanding of criticism. Allowance must be made for the date of the translations, e.g. in Campion 'sager' and 'weigh' may be quite natural expressions but 'Heaven's great lamps do dive ...' seems a wordy and inadequate

rendering of Catullus and misses the point of **occidere**, which means at once 'to set' and 'to die'.

Poem 43

1 **salve**: an ironical greeting; the celebration of a girl's beauty is turned upside down in this poem.

Poem 109

This is the second poem in which Catullus refers to himself and his mistress as **nos**, but significantly in l. 3 the person changes to 'she'. Your students should notice this.

6 **aeternam ... amicitiae**: 'this eternal compact of hallowed friendship' (Wiseman). Catullus saw their love in a very different light from Clodia, who, he knows in his heart, will not prove capable of keeping such a compact, whatever promises she may make (see p. 26, fourth paragraph, above).

Poem 70

This may have been written before or after the death of Metellus, Clodia's husband. If before, divorce was easy enough in Rome. The form of the poem owes much to an epigram by Callimachus (*Ep.* 25), but whereas Callimachus is light-hearted and ironical about the promises of lovers, Catullus is deadly serious.

Poem 72

'These four patiently argued couplets are remarkable no less for their clarity of insight than for their precise formulation of a lost ideal' (Quinn).

3–4 **dilexi ... generos**: see comments on p. 26 above.

5 **nunc te cognovi**: 'now I have got to know you, found you out'.

Poem 85

The theme of the disillusioned lover is a familiar one in poetry, but the directness and stark simplicity of Catullus' couplet are unique – and shattering. Fénelon writes of 'ces paroles négligées où le coeur saisi parle seul dans une espèce de désespoir'.

2 **excrucior**: the word is derived from **crux** and suggests crucifixion, perhaps the most horrible of Roman punishments

Poem 8

An internal dialogue in which Catullus determines to put an intense love affair behind him. He sees his folly

(l. 1) but is trapped by his obsession. The seven imperatives through which he stresses his resolve (ll. 9, 10, 11, 12, 19) plus the two jussive subjunctives (ll. 1–2) accumulate with such over-emphasis that they may in themselves cause us to question the poet's ability to break free.

The poem starts as a soliloquy in which Catullus exhorts himself to stop being a fool. He looks back on the sunlit past of their love with infinite sadness, but then pulls himself up and tells himself to harden his heart. The second section is addressed to his girl – when Catullus leaves her she will be sorry – but the series of questions becomes increasingly emotional as they recall his own past love. In the last line he again pulls himself up – he must forget these thoughts and be strong.

Throughout the poem runs the antithesis between Catullus' intellectual decision to leave his mistress and his emotional inability to do so.

The poem is in limping iambics: elsewhere, apart from one poem of apparently unclouded joy (31 – see p. 132), Catullus uses this metre to convey violently scornful attacks on his enemies. Here we find this sour tone in the attack on the girl in ll. 15–18, but the limping iambics have another effect in the rest of the poem. The constantly surprising long penultimate syllables in each line undermine the smoothness of the iambics in the first five feet. They register a kick against the established rhythm, and this adds a repeated note of poignancy. In addition, the poet's use of this metre enables him to have a spondee at the end of the line, which proves particularly effective in suggesting the desperate need for steadfastness (**obdura**, ll. 11 and 19; cf. l. 12).

Poem 76

1–8 the poem appears to start calmly as Catullus reassures himself that he will have consolation, since he has been *pius*, has kept the *foedus* he made with his mistress, and done and said all that any man could. But Catullus is developing an old commonplace: see e.g. Cicero: *de Senectute* 9: *aptissima omnino sunt arma senectutis artes exercitationesque virtutum ... conscientia bene actae vitae multorumque benefactorum recordatio iucundissima est* ('the most appropriate weapons of old age are the study and practice of the virtues ... because the consciousness of a life well led and the memory of many good deeds is most pleasant').

The conditional in ll. 1–2 (**si qua ... voluptas est homini**) points the irony and bitterness which underlie his statement of a well-worn theme.

9–16: the emotional intensity rises as he argues with himself in his efforts to shake off this love. We know that he cannot do it.

17–26: at l. 17 he bursts into a desperate prayer to the gods to tear from him this destructive plague; now he only wishes to be free.

Poem 77

There may not be time to treat the topic of Clodia and Caelius fully but it might be worth translating poem 77 and the passage from the *pro Caelio*.
1 **Rufe**: the identification of Rufus with M. Caelius Rufus is not universally accepted; there are other poems to a Rufus (69 and 71) who had smelly armpits and does not sound a bit like the fashionable Caelius. But as Caelius did succeed Catullus as one of Lesbia's (= Clodia's) lovers, it seems extremely plausible that he is the subject of this poem.

pro Caelio 49–50

The prosecution was brought by L. Sempronius Atratinus, whose father Caelius had prosecuted the year before, in April 56 BC. The charge was riot (*de vi*). But whatever the technical charges were, it is clear that Clodia was the driving force behind the prosecution and that the case was brought from personal motives.

Illustrations

p. 115: this vividly painted sparrow is a wall painting from the Roman villa at Oplontis. See note on the illustration on p. 15 (p. 7 above).
p. 118: this terracotta figure of a standing woman was made in Boeotia c. 300–200 BC; it is said to be from Tanagra. (British Museum, London)
p. 119: this Hellenistic sculpture shows Cupid embracing Psyche. It is in the Capitoline Museum in Rome and is thus popularly known as the Capitoline Kiss.
p. 127: this small statue of Cupid astride a dolphin has a Hellenistic prettiness and probably dates from the first century BC. (British Museum, London)

3 The sequel

Poems 11, 46, 101, 31, 4, 10

Poem 11

This, which is generally considered the last of the Lesbia poems, is written in sapphics, the metre Catullus used for poem 51 (see p. 29 above), which is believed by many to be the first.

The poem is cunningly constructed with two

violent changes of direction and shifts in tone. The romantic travelogue (ll. 1–12) leads the reader, or listener, up the garden path; he can have no idea of what is to follow **temptare simul parati** (l. 14); the most dangerous mission of all turns out to be **pauca nuntiate meae puellae** (l. 15). The vast Roman world narrows down to a short journey through its capital, and it is not until the next line that we find out why this mission is so dangerous.

The fifth stanza gives the message in terms of bitter contempt, in which sound effects are expressive of the sense: alliteration – **vivat valeatque, tenet trecentos** – and in the following line three elisions of syllables ending in **m**, one over the end of the line (a rare licence): **nullum amans vere, sed identidem omnium ...** The interpretation of such an effect is apt to be subjective but to our ear it is extremely ugly, a sort of slimy slur.

In the last stanza there comes another complete shift in tone, as he looks back on his love as a thing of beauty, carelessly, almost negligently cut down by her fault. Here there is a sound effect – the elision of **prati** over the end of the line – of which we can speak more confidently; the cutting of the syllable expresses the cutting off of the flower.

1 **Furi et Aureli**: other poems make it clear that Catullus has very little respect for Furius and Aurelius.

11 **horribile aequor**: the MSS read **horribilesque ulti-**; this gives a very violent hiatus after **-que**, but perhaps it is the correct reading.

22–3 **prati ultimi**: why 'the edge of the meadow'? The flower – and the love – might have escaped the plough.

Poem 46

Structure: ll. 1–6: spring is here; it's time to be off; ll. 7–11: I long to start; friends, goodbye. The linking line, in our view, is l. 7 (**ad claras ... volemus**). Our reason for preferring this interpretation to that of e.g. Quinn lies in the sound echoes:

> **iam ver egelidos refert tepores** (l. 1)
> **iam mens praetrepidans avet vagari** (l. 7)

(apart from the sound echoes in the first two words of each line, the lines are rhythmically identical)

> **iam caeli ...** (l. 2)
> **iam laeti ...** (l. 8)

Catullus' state of mind echoes the state of the season – new growth, new beginning after storms. A poem of joy and relief, just tinged with sadness at the end, as he will miss his friends.

Poem 101

We learn from poem 68 (ll. 89–96) that Catullus' brother died at Troy:

> Troia (nefas!) commune sepulcrum Asiae
> Europaeque,
> Troia virum et virtutum omnium acerba cinis,
> quaene etiam nostro letum miserabile fratri
> attulit. ei misero frater adempte mihi,
> ei misero fratri iucundum lumen ademptum,
> tecum una tota est nostra sepulta domus,
> omnia tecum una perierunt gaudia nostra,
> quae tuus in vita dulcis alebat amor.

> Troy (what wickedness!) the shared grave of Asia
> and Europe,
> Troy the bitter ashes of men and of all manly
> qualities,
> Troy which also brought lamentable death to my
> brother.
> Alas, brother stolen from me in my pitiful state,
> alas the pleasant light of life stolen from my pitiful
> brother;
> our whole house is buried with you,
> all our joys have perished along with you,
> joys which your sweet love fed while you lived.

The strength of poem 101 is partly due to the directness of the thought and the dignified simplicity of the language. When you read the last of the Ovid poems, the elegy on Tibullus (p. 220), it would be instructive to compare the two poems. Ovid's elegy is another powerful expression of grief, more complex in thought and more decorated in expression.

Poem 31

For Catullus' tour of duty on the staff of the governor of Bithynia, see p. 128 of the Reader.

Poem 31 is called by Merrill (1893) 'a most unartificial and joyous pouring out of feeling' (see question 4). Certainly no reader could fail to respond to the joy and relief expressed in the central part of the poem in the most natural language. But the poem is not entirely 'unartificial'. The first three lines are sophisticated in expression, especially in the conceit of **uterque Neptunus** (l. 3), which probably means 'Neptune in both his capacities', i.e. as god of fresh water and god of the salt sea; and at the end we have another piece of artificiality in **o Lydiae lacus undae** (l. 13); Wiseman (p. 110) suggests that as the Roman colonists were comparatively recent, they equipped themselves with a legendary past to express their pride in their new country. Certainly the language of the opening and ending is different from that of the central section, more elevated and poetic, perhaps; twice in the last three lines we find **o**, which is used in Latin only in passages of strong emotion. The only other artificiality occurs in ll. 5–6: **Thyniam atque Bithynos ... campos**, which appears to be a piece of word play; Herodotus

(1.28) refers to the Thynoi and Bithynoi as Thracian tribes living in Lydia but the area was known only as Bithynia in Catullus' time. The Greek prefix *bi-* leads to the playful assumption that if there was a Bithynia, there must be a Thynia too.

Poem 4

This is a variation on a regular type of Hellenistic poem that records the dedication to a god of the tools of a man's trade which have served their turn. There are many of these in the *Greek Anthology*.

Catullus had visited the province of Bithynia and Pontus in 57/6 BC (poem 10), he visited the Troad (poem 101) and he expressed his intention to fly (46.6) to the famous cities of Asia on his way home. He memorably encapsulates the joy of homecoming to Sirmio on Lake Garda in poem 31. This is the the the journey which he describes both backwards (ll. 6–9) and forwards (ll. 17–24) in poem 4.

To literal-minded objections, say to the problem of Catullus' sailing a sea-going yacht up to Po and Mincio to Lake Garda, Frank O. Copley provides a sane solution, writing that poem 4 'is not a piece of autobiography even if it is autobiographical. That is to say, it was not written to recount an incident of the poet's life, even if its data were drawn from his experiences.'

The personification of the retired yacht is a lively one. A pensioner's loquacity as he relives the great days of old is its most notable feature. There are verbs of speaking in ll. 2, 6, 12, 15 and 16 and the bulk of the poem is in indirect statement. Perhaps we are meant to recall the most famous ship of epic, the *Argo*, which, like Catullus' yacht, could talk.

The poem is a metrical *tour de force*; to write pure iambics (with no use of spondees) in a language as heavy as Latin requires extraordinary skill and yet it reads as if it were the easiest thing in the world.

Poem 10

This is the best example of Catullus' mastery of the use of colloquial diction in verse; throughout the poem we feel the language and rhythms of rather racy everyday speech. The only Roman poet to manage this skill so well was Horace in some of his *Satires* and *Epistles* (e.g. *Satires* 1.5 and 9; see Part III, chs 44 and 45). 33–4 **sed tu ...**: there was no punctuation in Roman writing. Did the poet speak these last two lines out loud, or did he say them to himself? Ask your students what they think.

Illustrations

p. 128: a Scythian bronze of a backward-shooting Parthian rider (a characteristic tactic, and the basis for our expression 'Parthian shot'). (British Museum, London)

p. 130 (above): St Paul's Christian teaching in this Hellenistic theatre (with a capacity of 24,000) sparked off a serious demonstration (Acts 19:22ff.). The tradition goes that he was put in a prison on the hill to the left. The road leads down to what was once a thriving harbour, but the sea has receded.

(below): inside the east gate at Troy (Troy VI, 1800–1275 BC). This is thought to be the Troy of Priam's era. A curving passage between two walls leads to the gate (behind the photographer). Any attackers would find themselves confined in a narrow space and be forced to withstand a barrage from above. The excavations of the German Heinrich Schliemann between 1870 and 1890 wreaked vast havoc on the site, but some of his work has left imposing results, such as this gate. It lay buried when Byron, visiting the area, wrote to Henry Drury: 'The Troad [the plain of Troy] is a fine field for conjecture and Snipe-shooting, and a good sportsman and an ingenious scholar may exercise their feet and faculties upon the spot, or if they prefer losing their way (as I did) in a cursed quagmire of the Scamander [one of the rivers of Troy] who wriggles about as if the Dardan virgins still offered their wonted tribute ... Mt Ida is still in high feather, though the Shepherds are nowadays not much like Ganymede.'

p. 131: a wall painting from Pompeii. (National Archaeological Museum, Naples)

p. 136: this sculpture of Jupiter Serapis dates from the second century AD. It was found in Rome in 1775 and is now in the British Museum.

Virgil

Chapter 1 consists of excerpts from Book 1 of the *Aeneid*, chapters 2 and 3 of excerpts from Book 4. A good modern edition of *Aeneid* 1–6 is that edited by R. D. Williams, Macmillan. R. G. Austin's editions of Books 1 and 4, Oxford, are highly recommended. See also T. E. Page's edition of *Aeneid* 1–6, Macmillan. From the vast range of books on the *Aeneid*, the following are by no means exclusive recommendations:

W. A Camps: *An Introduction to Virgil's Aeneid*, Oxford
K. W. Gransden: *Virgil: The Aeneid*, Cambridge
J. Griffin: *Virgil* (Past Masters series), Oxford
P. R. Hardie: *Virgil's Aeneid: Cosmos and Imperium*, Oxford

S. J. Harrison, ed.: *Oxford Readings in Virgil's Aeneid*, Oxford

R. Jenkyns: *Classical Epic: Homer and Virgil*, Bristol Classical Press

B. Otis: *Virgil: A Study in Civilized Poetry*, Oxford

K. Quinn: *Virgil's Aeneid: A Critical Description*, Routledge & Kegan Paul

The political dimension of Virgil's work has been discussed at some length earlier in the course.

We have sketched in the crucially important relationship of Virgil to Homer in Part I of the course (pp. 64–5). The correspondences and dissimilarities between the epics of Homer and Virgil are a fertile field for debate, and they are of course much more complicated than we have suggested on those pages, for Virgil makes copious use of Homer's language as well as his themes. A valuable book here is R. Jenkyns' *Classical Epic: Homer and Virgil*.

There are further debts. We give here the story of Dido and Aeneas, which Virgil did not invent but treated with unprecedented depth and pathos. The most important sources for this part of the poem are **1** Apollonius of Rhodes, who wrote with sensitivity and intensity of the love of Medea for Jason in his *Argonautica (The Voyage of the Argo*, third century BC), **2** Catullus, who had responded with a poignant sense of personal involvement to the situation of Ariadne abandoned by Theseus (Poem 64), and **3** Euripides with his portrayals of wild emotion and his mastery of feminine psychology. For the story of Dido and Aeneas, recent history provided a parallel, since, as Augustan propaganda had it, the fatal oriental queen Cleopatra enslaved and destroyed the great Roman leader Mark Antony.

Virgil wrote the *Aeneid* between 29 and 19 BC. He died before he could finally revise it. (For the Virgilian hexameter, see Appendix 2 of the Reader.)

The term 'Golden Age' in the introduction (p. 140) refers to Latin literature from 100 BC to the death of Livy (AD 17).

1 Aeneas arrives at Carthage

Aeneid 1.12–22, 29–33, 338–66, 418–38, 494–508

Introductory passage (p. 142): you may wish to tell your pupils the story of the Trojan horse.

1 antiqua: the city of Carthage is still being built when Aeneas reaches North Africa. Thus it is **antiqua** not from Aeneas' point of view but from that of Virgil. At many points in the *Aeneid*, Virgil makes such use of 'double time', viewing events both as they occur in his narrative and as they appear in the context of Augustan Rome. Between the times of Aeneas and Virgil the Punic Wars had been fought between Carthage and Rome, ending in the total destruction of Carthage in 146 BC. Interestingly, however, Carthage was being rebuilt as a Roman colony while Virgil was writing the *Aeneid*.

2–3 Italiam ... Tiberinaque ... ostia: as we suggest in our gloss, this means 'Italy where the Tiber runs into the sea' rather than 'Italy *and* the mouth of the Tiber'. This kind of phrase, where the second unit explains the first, is common in Virgil and other Latin poets.

Tiberina ... ostia: 'the mouth of the Tiber' but also Ostia, the harbour located there.

4–5 quam Iuno ...: Juno's love for Carthage is due to the fact that she was worshipped there as the goddess Tanit.

11 Parcas: the three Fates were Clotho (the Spinner – hence **volvere**), Atropos and Lachesis. What is fated in the *Aeneid* will happen but it can be delayed or modified. Vulcan tells Venus that he could have made the Trojan War last for another ten years; neither the Fates nor Jupiter would have stopped him (8.398–9).

16 tantae molis erat ...: a famous line. The labour and suffering involved in establishing the Roman race are repeatedly stressed in the poem.

Romanam condere gentem: this is Aeneas' destiny.

22 ditissimus agri: **agri** is a Greek genitive, variously called the genitive of 'respect' or 'sphere in which'.

27 furor: a key concept in the poem: it is opposed by *pietas*, the quality possessed above all by Aeneas.

28–30 impius ... germanae: see last note. The impiety of Pygmalion is stressed both by the scene of the murder (**ante aras**) and by his violation of the family bond in killing his sister's husband.

29 securus amorum: securus ('unconcerned about') is regularly followed by the genitive. **amorum** is a 'poetic plural', lending importance to Dido's love (cf. note on l. 109, p. 39 below)

32 inhumati: the impious Pygmalion has not even buried his victim. Without burial, the spirits of the dead could not find rest.

34 crudelis: this is the first instance we have met of a 3rd declension accusative plural ending in **-is** instead of **-es**. This occurs very frequently.

39 fugam ... sociosque parabat: a good example of syllepsis. The verb has its literal meaning with one of its objects and a non-literal meaning with the other: cf. 'He lost his hat and his temper.' In English syllepsis is often used to humorous effect, but rarely so in Latin.

43 dux femina facti: throughout this passage (ll. 19–45), Virgil has shown to what extent Dido is an *alter Aeneas* (a second Aeneas). They have both lost their partners in marriage; both of them, warned by a ghost in a dream, have fled from a city where there is no future for them, showing outstanding courage and leadership. Aeneas wishes to found a new city; Dido is already founding one. With so much in common, it is not surprising that they are attracted to each other.

49–50 miratur ... miratur: Aeneas is suitably impressed by the construction of the city. City-building is an important theme of the poem; **magalia** is a Carthaginian word. T. E. Page suggests that 'Virgil is probably thinking of the view of Rome from the Esquiline, from the palace from which Horace tells us that Maecenas loved *mirari beatae/fumum et opes strepitumque Romae* (*Odes* 3.29.11–12)'.

54 senatum: Carthage had a senate from about 400 BC, but the civilized order shown in Dido's projected city indicates that Virgil is creating an ideal picture rather than trying to describe the beginnings of the real Carthage. It is the city of Aeneas' dreams.

58–64 qualis apes ...: Virgil elsewhere uses bees to convey a co-operative and happy community. See *Georgics* 4 *passim* and *Aeneid* 6.707–9. Brooks Otis remarks that 'the simile suggests all the sweetness of security and happy employment' and W. R. Johnson finds in it an expression of Virgil's 'own best dream, the unity of the City'. Similes were established by Homer as an important ingredient of epic.

65 o fortunati ...: 'The want of a city is the keynote of the *Aeneid*' (Conington).

71–5 qualis in Eurotae ...: the simile is based on Homer: *Odyssey* 6.102ff. It is altogether joyous, but note that Diana **pharetram/fert umero**; i.e. she is a huntress. Dido, on the other hand, is to prove the victim of the hunt.

78 foribus divae: the doors of the shrine (*cella*) at the back of the temple's main hall which has a vaulted roof (**testudine**).

Illustrations

p. 140: this bust, possibly of Virgil, is in the Capitoline Museum at Rome.

p. 142: Juno holds a sceptre in her right hand and a phial in her left. The statue is known as the Hera Barberini and was found on the Viminal hill in the seventeenth century.

p. 143 (above): the baths complex at Tyre. This important city in southern Phoenicia, built on an island but extending ashore, was equipped with two harbours.

(below): the Vatican Library has in its collection the two earliest illustrated manuscripts of Virgil, both dating from the close of the classical period. This illustration of the storm comes from the later of them, the Codex Romanus (fifth or sixth century AD). Close to despair, Aeneas stretches forth his arms as malign figures shower rain and lightning from above. Beady-

eyed sea monsters gleefully await their prey.

p. 144: this illustration from the earlier (fourth-century) Vatican manuscript, the Codex Vaticanus, shows Aeneas with his friend Achates gazing in wonder at the building of Carthage. The wheel is part of a crane (*machina*, p. 148, l. 30).

p. 146 (above): the bee is on a silver coin minted at Ephesus between 387 and 295 BC.

(below): from the Codex Romanus, the later Vatican manuscript. Dido reclines on a semi-circular couch between Aeneas (on the left) and Achates. The Trojans wear Phrygian caps and purple robes. The haloes show a curious melding of Christian and pagan art.

p. 147: this statue is a copy of a work by the Greek master Praxiteles (active c. 375–330 BC). Over Cupid's quiver we see draped the lion skin of Hercules: this small boy can wreak as much damage as the strongest hero of antiquity. (Capitoline Museum, Rome)

2 The love of Dido and Aeneas

Aeneid 4.1–5, 65–89, 129–36, 138–72, 259–86, 305–30

1–2 at regina ...: Cupid's traditional weapons are arrows (causing the wound of love) and fire (representing the flames of passion). At the end of Book 4, Dido stabs herself and then (5.2–3) is consumed by the flames of a pyre. The metaphors become realities.

iamdudum: Dido has in fact fallen in love very quickly, through divine intervention; the use of this word conveys her impression that her love for Aeneas has already lasted a long time; **cura** suggests the anxious pain of love. Throughout the book, Virgil presents Dido's love as a torment, as something that consumes her. Contrast the usual modern view of love (propagated above all by Shakespeare) as life-enhancing.

5 nec ... dat cura: be careful not to allow **nec** to be translated as 'nor', which will lead to translator's language and not real English: 'and her suffering withholds ...'.

6–8 heu ... vulnus: the prophets and the rituals Dido performs are useless. Her suffering lies deep within her. The ideas of fire (**flamma**) and the wound (**vulnus**) should be stressed; **tacitum vulnus:** Cf.. *Hamlet* 1.2: 'But break my heart for I must hold my tongue.'

10–14 qualis ...: analysis of this celebrated simile must not do less than justice to its pathos and its evocation of pain. Note its location in the cold and wild uplands of Crete. Aeneas is the shepherd who is out hunting. (Is there a contradiction between the roles of shepherd and hunter?) He shoots an arrow at a doe he is pursuing and is unaware that it has hit her. (Is Aeneas in any way guilty?) The doe is Dido, caught off her guard, shot, and then roaming restlessly over the mountain slopes in dreadful agony. The **sagitta** is the arrow of love which cannot be removed (**haeret**). Matthew Arnold poignantly evokes this simile in *Sohrab and Rustum* 503–6:

> most like the roar
> Of some pain'd desert-lion, who all day
> Hath trail'd the hunter's javelin in his side,
> And comes at night to die upon the sand.

13 silvas saltusque: hendiadys; i.e. the two nouns suggest one idea, 'the wooded defiles'. Cf. 'bread and butter'. Explain this to your pupils.

22 luna ... premit: this evocative line should be scanned and its sound savoured. The last three words form a beautiful cadence with ictus (the stress dictated by scansion) coinciding with speech stress. See Appendix 2 of the Reader.

25 Ascanium: the real Ascanius has now replaced the disguised Cupid.

29–30 pendent opera ...: all work on the city has stopped. The crane simply standing there idle is an evocative symbol of suspended activity. Dido's private passion has taken her over: it has eclipsed her public *persona* as queen of Carthage. The contrast with the **dux femina facti** of Book 1 should be stressed.

31 Oceanum: the river Oceanus emerged from the underworld and flowed about the earth which was conceived as flat (like a plate).

33 retia: in a Roman hunt, nets were set up at the far side of the hunting area; the quarry was driven into these and killed.

There is no verb in this line. The gear comes (**it**, l. 32) out at the gates with the young men. The poet's eye leaps excitedly from item to item. Encourage your pupils to translate one 'period' at a time. This is the secret of reading Virgil.

34 canum vis: the monosyllable at the end of the line dislocates the cadence and conveys an impression of bustling activity which is well in keeping with the animation of this passage as a whole. See Appendix 2 of the Reader.

35 reginam ...: Dido lingers in her bedroom with the bashfulness of a bride about to set off for her marriage.

42 nec non et 'and ... as well'. **Iulus** and **Ascanius** are names used interchangeably of Aeneas' son.

44–50 qualis ...: this simile likening Aeneas to Apollo looks back to the simile comparing Dido with Apollo's sister Diana (ch. 1, ll. 71–5). The summer setting with the jovial noise of an international festival and the splendid appearance of Apollo himself create a heady impression. But note the sinister effect of the weapons

sounding on Apollo's shoulder (Cf. Homer: *Iliad* 1.45–7). Aeneas and the arrow of love are to prove fatal to Dido. The picture of Apollo balances delicacy with power.

It was traditional to use similes to characterize. Cf. the simile by which Jason is introduced when meeting Medea in the *Argonautica* of Apollonius (3.956–61):

> She longed to see him, and he soon appeared to her, his tall figure springing into view like the dog-star Sirius coming from the Ocean. The star rises beautiful and clear to behold but brings unspeakable woe to the animals. Thus Jason came to her, beautiful to look on, but his appearance aroused the torments of love.

55–6 transmittunt ... relinquunt: to an English-speaking reader it appears that Virgil is saying that the deer first career over the plains and *then* quit the mountains – which is clearly not his meaning. Virgil's descriptive technique is not sequential but cumulative.

57–60 at puer Ascanius ...: Aeneas is about to embark on a love affair which is to put his son's dynastic future at risk. It is appropriate that Ascanius should be presented here as the epitome of mettlesome youth.

61ff. interea ...: the storm is emblematic of the forces of *furor* in the world (cf. 1.148–56).

66 dux: the use of the word is devastating. By his union with Dido, Aeneas effectively abandons his leadership of his men. He becomes Dido's consort. He *leads* Dido into the cave; and she persuades herself that he is her bridegroom (**duco** can mean 'I marry').

67ff. prima et Tellus ...: 'The elemental powers of nature and supernatural divinities conspire to produce a parody of a wedding, a hallucination by which the unhappy Dido is deceived' (Williams). Cf. Milton's fine lines when Eve eats the apple (*Paradise Lost* 9.782–4):

> Earth felt the wound, and Nature from her seate Sighing through all her Works gave signs of woe, That all was lost.

73 coniugium vocat ...: on his side, Aeneas has made no commitment.

74 alatis: Mercury wears winged sandals.

75 fundantem ... novantem: work has started up again. But it is not Carthage that Aeneas should be building.

76–9 atque illi ...: this oriental picture of Aeneas, wearing a cloak made for him by Dido, gives an effeminate impression. He is neglecting his Roman duty.

77 Tyrio murice: Tyrian dye, which produced a glowing purple colour, was made from an extract from a vein of the whelk (**murex** 'a shellfish'). It was very expensive, with some 12,000 whelks being needed to produce 1.5 grams of fluid.

81 uxorius: Mercury is being highly contemptuous.

82 regni rerumque ... tuarum: i.e. Aeneas' Roman and Italian destiny.

86: note the jingle of **teris** and **terris**: does this convey the idea of lingering? Contempt is surely present.

95 ardet abire: after his initial shock – on which Virgil focuses arrestingly – Aeneas is on fire to leave, and quickly (**fuga**). But note that the land of Carthage is still sweet (**dulcis**) to him.

97–8 agat ... audeat ... sumat: deliberative subjunctives.

99–100 animum ... versat: Aeneas' mental *impasse* is strikingly conveyed. Cf. Tennyson's 'this way and that dividing the swift mind'.

101–26 dissimulare ...: the enormous range of emotions spanned in this speech calls for discussion. You might ask your pupils if they feel that it is very much a woman's speech and, if so, why?

124 parvulus: the only example of a diminutive adjective in the *Aeneid*. It creates an effect of extraordinary intimacy with the non-existent child.

Illustrations

p. 148 (above): this mosaic of a deer, dating from about the third century AD, is from a Roman villa at Sousse in Tunisia. (Sousse Museum)

(below): this hunter is painted on an Attic red-figure vase (a *lekythos*), the work of the Pan Painter, dating from c. 470–460 BC. (The Francis Bartlett Fund, Museum of Fine Arts, Boston)

p. 150 (above): a detail from a sarcophagus in the Museo Nazionale, Rome.

(below): this mosaic of a hunt (from a series of hunting scenes) is from the vast Roman villa at Piazza Armerina in Sicily. It dates from the first three decades of the fourth century AD and is of the Romano-African school. The mosaics from this villa form what is probably the finest ensemble in this art form surviving from the ancient world.

p. 152: from the later Vatican manuscript, which is more cartoon-like than the earlier one. As the royal couple make love in a cave, two fellow-hunters shelter under a tree and a shield respectively. One of the horses looks anxiously upward.

p. 153: this relief from a Roman marble sarcophagus of the second century AD shows the Roman marriage ceremony of *dextrarum iunctio*. In their left hands, the bride holds a rose and the husband the wedding contract. Behind them stands the bridesmaid. (British Museum, London)

p. 154: this Giam Bologna (1529–1608) statue of Mercury is Renaissance in period but classical in feeling. He has wings on his hat and his ankles and he holds his caduceus, a winged staff with two serpents twining round it. (Louvre Museum, Paris)

p. 156: the council chamber (*bouleuterion*) at Troy dates from the time of the early Roman empire. It is a theatre, the lowest row of whose seating is of marble, which was originally enclosed within square outer walls to serve as a meeting place for the councillors of the Hellenistic city.

p. 157: the mosaic floor of the *frigidarium* from Low Ham in Somerset (fourth century AD). You can now review the story so far; it is told anti-clockwise from the bottom right: (a) Aeneas' ships arrive at the coast of Africa; (b) Venus and Cupid (disguised as Ascanias) supervise the meeting of Dido and Aeneas; (c) they go hunting; Aeneas looks back at Dido while Ascanius rushes ahead; (d) they make love. At the centre, Venus is flanked by two Cupids holding lowered and raised torches, symbolizing the death of Dido and the continuing life of Aeneas respectively. (Achates, holding a gift for Dido, appears to be on his back at the top right; in fact, he belongs to the group (b).) The Trojans wear Phrygian hats.

3 The death of Dido

Aeneid 4.330–61, 393–415, 607–29, 642–705

2 obnixus: Virgil tells us that it was an effort for Aeneas to stifle his love.

3ff. ego te ...: we quote two extreme views of this, the only speech of Aeneas in Book 4: 'Not all Virgil's art can make the figure of Aeneas here appear other than despicable. His conduct had been vile, and Dido's heart-broken appeal brings its vileness into strong relief' (Page). 'Virgil has taken the utmost care to convey the reasons why Aeneas' reply is cold; it is [1–2] because he knows he must not yield and therefore he smothers his love and his emotions. He endeavours to use logical and persuasive arguments to put his case, honestly believing that Dido will see that he has no option' (Williams).

ego te: 'the two persons concerned face each other syntactically, as it were' (Austin).

7 pro re pauca loquar: usually taken to mean 'I shall speak a few words to meet the case', and this is certainly in keeping with the formal, legalistic tone of the speech. But Aeneas could be saying, 'In proportion to (the greatness of) the matter, I shall speak (only) a few words', i.e. he could be acknowledging the magnitude of what is happening.

7–8 neque ego ...: would there in fact ever have been a right time or a right way for Aeneas to break the news to Dido?

10–14 me si ...: Aeneas points out chillingly that if he had his way he would rebuild Troy rather than stay with Dido. This is an arresting statement of the city-building theme.

Priami tecta alta manerent: i.e. he would build Priam's palace again on the ruins of the old one.

15–16, 21–3: we have not heard about these oracles or the appearances of Anchises' ghost before now.

28–9 ipse ... hausi: Mercury appeared to him in person, not in a dream. He stresses this fact.

31 Italiam non sponte sequor: Virgil would have completed this and the other half-lines in the poem if he had lived to finish the poem. 'Nothing ...', writes Page, 'could improve these four words thus left rugged and abrupt.' But how could Page, or anyone else for that matter, know that Virgil could not in fact have improved on them?

32 pius: now that Aeneas is acting in accordance with his destiny, he can have his epithet of **pius** restored to him. It has not been used since 1.378 (this is 4.393). His *pietas* is the reason for – indeed the only justification for – his departure. There is a sense in which Virgil is here emptying the word **pius** of any laudatory or condemnatory associations. He is simply telling us the fundamental truth about the man we now see. Ask your pupils how they respond to this word at this stage of the story.

34 multa gemens ...: Virgil again (cf. l. 2) assures us that Aeneas' feelings were profound, but these almost editorial statements do not carry as great a weight as words and deeds. In fact, we see into Dido's heart in this book in a way that is almost completely denied us in the case of Aeneas. (But see 4.441–9.)

animum labefactus: animum is a retained accusative with the passive verb used in a middle sense.

35 iussa tamen divum: in embracing the orders of the gods, Aeneas shows himself to be a true Stoic.

37 carina: 'The use of the singular here gives a sudden picture of one of the many ships as it is launched' (Williams).

38–9 frondentisque ... studio: it is a curious accident that the second of these lines about incomplete oars was itself left incomplete at Virgil's death.

40 cernas: 'you would have seen them' (a potential subjunctive). The present tense is used to add vividness and immediacy.

41–6 ac velut ...: the simile Virgil uses elsewhere in the poem to suggest a happily co-operative community, that of bees in a sunlit and flowering countryside (ch. 1, ll. 58–64; 6.707–9), is here transformed into a description of efficient ants. Effortfully provident as ants proverbially are, they summon up a picture of communal discipline for Dido and for us to behold. It is in this bleak light that we are asked at this moment to view the destiny of Rome.

43 it ... herbas: a good line to demonstrate the clash of ictus with speech stress (see Appendix 2 of the Reader). There is a sense of laborious trudging. Ennius used *it nigrum campis agmen* of elephants.

44 grandia: i.e. from the point of view of the ants.

47 quis tibi ...: Virgil addresses one of his characters in the second person. This is a device called apostrophe (the poet 'turns away from' his narrative). Here it indicates his profound sympathy for Dido.

49 arce ex summa: Dido stands on her lonely height. Far below, the Trojans do indeed look like ants.

51 improbe Amor: in a second apostrophe, Virgil addresses the god of love. How effective does this prove? Does it intensify the emotional effect or weaken it by protesting too much?

55 Sol: the sun sees everything: nothing can be hidden from it. Dido invokes it as a witness of Aeneas' treachery.

56 conscia Iuno: she speaks more truly than she knows. For Juno's role in furthering the liaison between Dido and Aeneas, see p. 148. From the reader's point of view, though not from Dido's, **interpres** may here come close to meaning 'bawd'.

57 Hecate: she was worshipped at the crossroads.

60ff. si tangere portus ...: Virgil modelled these curses on Polyphemus' curse upon Odysseus in *Odyssey* 9.532ff., another tale of violated hospitality. The Polyphemus story is very different, but there are some instructive comparisons to be made. While Dido's curses were all fulfilled, some do not happen in the *Aeneid*. The educated Roman reader was expected to have picked up such information from his reading elsewhere.

Charles I was confronted by these terrible lines when he opened his Virgil in the 1640s. He was taking the *Sortes Vergilianae*. To do this, you open your Virgil suddenly; the passage you touch at random with your finger is the oracular response.

61 caput: denotes contempt.

70 vos, o Tyrii ...: she calls for undying enmity between Romans and Carthaginians.

71–2 cineri ... munera: cf. Catullus' poem about his brother's death (p. 131, poem 101, ll. 3–4).

73 aliquis ... ultor: this refers to Hannibal who came close to destroying Rome in 217 and 216 BC. The use of **aliquis** with the second person is startling. Dido cries out across the centuries with a passionate immediacy to someone she cannot know. The hissing 's's in this line are only one feature of a speech which contains many extraordinary sound effects.

76–7 litora litoribus ...: the idea of opposition is starkly reflected in the word order. The final **-que** goes over the end of the hexameter (i.e. is hypermetric). 'The never-ending hatred of Dido is reflected in the unended rhythm of her final words' (Williams). And Austin comments, more subjectively, 'Dido seems to leave the two peoples locked for ever in their enmity.'

79–80 trementis/interfusa genas: literally, 'blotched as to her quivering cheeks' – **trementis genas** is an accusative of respect.

82 gradus: a ladder leans against the pyre to enable Dido to climb to its top.

87 sinebat: the verb is singular because fate and god are viewed as a single concept.

88 exsolvite: Dido longs for release.

89ff. vixi ...: Heinze writes of Dido's 'echt römischer Heroismus' (truly Roman heroism). Like Horace's Cleopatra (*Odes* 1.37.30–34), Dido becomes the Stoic Roman in death. Her self-assertion has the simple dignity of inscriptions on tombstones.

90 magna ... imago: ghosts were thought to be larger than life – or perhaps Dido means that in her death she will achieve greatness.

91 urbem praeclaram statui: the city-building theme. In this line and the next, Dido reasserts her public self, looking back to the *alter Aeneas* theme.

92 ulta: how has she taken revenge upon her brother? She got away with her husband's hidden treasure, though it was partly for this that Pygmalion had killed him; she commandeered some of his ships; and she fled with a considerable number of dissidents (ch. 1, ll. 37–43).

94 carinae: synecdoche, the use of part of something to express the whole of it.

os impressa: os is a retained accusative with the passive verb used in a middle sense.

96 sic, sic: the ancient commentator Servius suggests that as she says **sic, sic**, Dido stabs herself twice. Shades of Bottom in *A Midsummer Night's Dream*! Surely Dido simply means, 'Thus, thus it is that I choose to die.'

105–7 non aliter quam ...: the simile of the sack of Carthage is a fine example of Virgil's use of double time. The poet makes his commentary on the ultimate failure of Dido's curse. The conflict between Carthage and Rome was to end with the sack of Carthage in 146 BC. The simile is based on *Iliad* 22.410. Austin comments that the sacking of a city was 'the most dreadful scene of horror that an ancient writer could imagine'. If we have read continuously through the poem, we still have in our mind the powerful description of the sack of Troy in Book 2.

109 ora ... pectora: these are 'poetic plurals'; i.e. the poet, as often, uses plurals where we would expect singulars. This is often due to the demands of metre, but there is usually some idea of mass or plurality, and it frequently happens with parts of the body, which are liable to come in pairs. We must translate the words in the singular. A number of these have been encountered in the course of the passage and it would be prudent to

make sure that the principle has been mastered.

111–12 hoc ... hoc: though nominative, **hoc** scans long in these lines. It should nevertheless be pronounced as a short vowel. See W. S. Allen: *Vox Latina*, Cambridge, pp. 76–7.

118–19 exstinxti ...: the enmity between Carthaginians and Romans which Dido had prayed for was to destroy her people in a way in which Anna could not anticipate. The Romans razed Carthage to the ground. Anna is presumably thinking of the defencelessness of Carthage against Pygmalion and the African tribes when the queen is dead. The educated reader would no doubt recall Andromache's lament for Hector in *Iliad* 24.725–45.

120–21 extremus ... legam: the soul was contained in the last breath of a dying man; the closest kinsman would try to catch it.

122 semianimem: scan as if the first 'i' were a 'j' (consonant).

124ff. illa, gravis ...: the composer Hector Berlioz who, in his great opera *The Trojans*, set Book 4 to music, writes memorably of his early response to Virgil: 'One day, I remember, I was disturbed from the outset of the lesson by the line:

> At regina gravi iamdumdum saucia cura.

Somehow or other I struggled on till we came to the great turning-point of the drama. But when I reached the scene in which Dido expires on the funeral pyre, surrounded by the gifts and weapons of the perfidious Aeneas, and pours forth on the bed – "that bed with all its memories" – the bitter stream of her life-blood, and I had to pronounce the despairing utterances of the dying queen, "thrice raising herself upon her elbow, thrice falling back", to describe her wound and the disastrous love that convulsed her to the depth of her being, the cries of her sister and her nurse and her distracted women, and that agony so terrible that the gods themselves are moved to pity and send Iris to end it, my lips trembled and the words came with difficulty, indistinctly. At last, at the line

> Quaesivit caelo lucem ingemuitque reperta

at that sublime image I was seized with a nervous shuddering and stopped dead. I could not have read another word.

'It was one of the occasions when I was most sensible of my father's unfailing goodness. Seeing how confused and embarrassed I was by such an emotion, but pretending not to have noticed anything, he rose abruptly and shut the book. "That will do, my boy," he said, "I'm tired." I rushed away, out of sight of everybody, to indulge my Virgilian grief.'

125 stridit: 'The word accurately expresses the whistling sound with which breath escapes from a pressed lung' (Mackail).

130 **difficilis obitus**: poetic plural.

131 **quae luctantem ...**: the metre of the line reflects
the tension followed by resolution.

132 **nec fato**: Dido was not fated to die so early and –
Virgil states the matter clearly – she did not deserve to
die (**merita nec morte**).

136ff. **ergo Iris ...**: the multicoloured Iris appears in
beauty and brings release to Dido at last. Do your
pupils feel that the Iris episode is the right way to end
this book? What are their reasons for their reactions?

At the start of Book 5, Aeneas sees flames rising from
Carthage. He does not know what they mean, but he
and his men feel a sense of foreboding. In Book 6 he
goes on a strange journey to the underworld and there
in the *lugentes campi*, where those whom love has
destroyed dwell, he meets Dido (*Aeneid* 6.450–76):

> Amongst them, with her death-wound still bleeding,
>   through the deep wood
> Was straying Phoenician Dido. Now when the
>   Trojan leader
> Found himself near her and knew that the form he
>   glimpsed through the shadows
> Was hers – as early in the month one sees, or
>   imagines he sees,
> Through a wrack of cloud the new moon rising and
>   glimmering –
> He shed some tears, and addressed her in tender,
>   loving tones: –
> Poor, unhappy Dido, so the message was true that
>   came to me
> Saying you'd put an end to your life with the sword
>   and were dead?
> Oh god! was it death I brought you, then? I swear
>   by the stars,
> By the powers above, by whatever is sacred in the
>   Underworld,
> It was not of my own will, Dido, I left your land.
> Heaven's commands, which now force me to
>   traverse the shades,
> This sour and derelict region, this pit of darkness,
>   drove me
> Imperiously from your side. I did not, could not
>   imagine
> My going would ever bring such terrible agony on
>   you.
> Don't move away! Oh, let me see you a little longer!
> To fly from me, when this is the last word fate
>   allows us!
> Thus did Aeneas speak, trying to soften the wild-
>   eyed,
> Passionate-hearted ghost, and brought the tears in
>   his own eyes.
> She would not turn to him; she kept her gaze on the
>   ground,

> And her countenance remained as stubborn to his
>   appeal
> As if it were carved from recalcitrant flint or a crag
>   of marble.
> At last she flung away, hating him still, and
>   vanished
> Into the shadowy wood where her first husband,
>   Sychaeus,
> Understands her unhappiness and gives her an equal
>   love.
> None the less did Aeneas, hard hit by her piteous
>   fate,
> Weep after her from afar, as she went, with tears of
>   compassion.

(translated by C. Day Lewis)

Illustrations

p. 158: Gian Lorenzo Bernini was only fifteen when he
sculpted this marble group jointly with his father in
1613. It shows the hero as he escapes from Troy,
carrying his father Anchises and leading his son
Ascanius by the hand. Anchises carries an image of the
goddess Vesta, Ascanius holds the sacred fire and
Aeneas wears a lion skin. This was a highly popular
subject in the ancient world. (Galleria Borghese, Rome)
p. 160: a cornelian gem of the first or second century
AD. (British Museum, London)
p. 162: this beautiful page of a manuscript of the late
fifteenth century shows Dido on her pyre as Aeneas
sails away. The prelude to the tragedy is shown: as the
hunt proceeds, Dido and Aeneas enter the cave. (British
Museum, London)
p. 166: this picture of Iris is from the Vatican Codex
Romanus.

Livy

With two exceptions, these chapters consist of excerpts
from Livy, Book 21. We think that pupils will probably
find Livy the most difficult of the writers in the Reader
and we have slimmed down the text substantially. Cuts
apart, we have altered nothing that he wrote and many
challenging passages remain. Livy's word order
frequently poses problems and you must stress how
vital it is to pay great attention to word endings. He
makes much use of the historic present and frequently
omits the verb 'to be'. The writing can be taut and
telegraphic, both vivid and dramatic. At other times, his
sentences come close to collapse. As L. P. Wilkinson
writes, 'he is apt to tack on participles, letting one

incident develop out of another as in real life; or to let a muddled sentence represent a confused scene.'

We refer readers to the admirable edition of Book 21 by P. G. Walsh, Bristol Classical Press. Other useful books are:

G. de Beer: *Hannibal*, Thames & Hudson

T. A. Dorey, ed.: *Livy*, Routledge & Kegan Paul

T. J. Luce: *Livy: The Composition of his History*, Princeton University Press

P. G. Walsh: *Livy* (Greece & Rome New Surveys in the Classics), Oxford

P. G. Walsh: *Livy: His Historical Aims and Methods*, Cambridge

A. J. Woodman and C. S. Kraus: *Latin Historians* (Greece & Rome New Surveys in the Classics), Oxford

Livy's relationship with Augustus (introduction, p. 168): Tacitus (*Annals* 4.34) tells how Livy praised Pompey so enthusiastically that Augustus called him 'the Pompeian', and how his republican sympathies led him to write of Cassius and Brutus, the assassins of Julius Caesar, with respect. It is possible that he regarded the rule of Augustus as necessary, but only as a short-term expedient. His comments on the study of history are from the Preface to Book 1.

1 Hannibal prepares to invade Italy

Book 21.1, 2, 4, 21, 27 and 28, with omissions

1 **praefari**: in addition to the Preface to the entire *History*, Livy wrote fresh introductions at suitable points. He wishes to stress the momentous nature of the Second Punic War (218–201 BC).

4–5 **neque validiores ... his ipsis**: here Livy consciously echoes Thucydides' preface to his history (1.1). Livy hoped to put his history on a level with that of his famous Greek predecessor. He aimed to write as definitive a history of Rome as Thucydides had of the Peloponnesian War, and he wanted to emphasize that he was part of a great tradition of historiography.

10–11 **inferrent, crederent**: subjunctives are regularly used to give a reported reason.

12 **fama**: the story appears in the work of Polybius (200–after 118 BC), the Greek historian whose work dealt with the rise of Rome to world power. He was one of Livy's main sources for the part of his history dealing with Hannibal. He in fact crossed the Alps in Hannibal's footsteps.

The episode Livy describes took place in 237 BC when Hannibal (247–183/2 BC) was nine.

17 **mors Hamilcaris**: Hamilcar died, by drowning, in 229/8 BC. Hasdrubal was in command in Spain until he was murdered in 221 BC.

25ff. **nunquam ingenium** ...: the character of Hannibal. Livy's model here is Sallust's portrait of Catiline (*Catiline* 14–16). It is a fine piece of writing: clauses and phrases are constantly balanced and alliteration (e.g. **perfidia plus quam Punica**, 1. 39) and the omission of verbs give the passage animation.

Summarizing Livy's character sketch of Hannibal, de Beer writes, 'Supreme at fighting, with a total disregard of danger, it is not surprising that all these qualities endeared him to his men to a fanatical extent.' According to Cornelius Nepos, Hannibal was a scholar as well as a soldier. There is no reason to believe that he was particularly treacherous or cruel (1. 39). As for piety (**nihil sancti**, 1. 39), an irreligious man does not travel more than 70 miles to worship his guardian diety as Hannibal did in 218 BC. Livy's description here reflects Roman bias.

43: we are now in January 218 BC.

59ff.: Hannibal's crossing probably took place at Fourques, opposite Arles. It was a sensational achievement. He crossed a river almost 1 km wide with 50,000 infantry, 9,000 cavalry and 37 elephants.

69 **ratibus iunctis**: the meaning given in the gloss seems the likely one, but the natural sense of the phrase suggests that they joined the rafts into larger units for the crossing, or made bridges of them.

76ff. **Galli** ...: Livy added this description of the Gauls to what he found in Polybius. His reading of Caesar may have inspired this lively passage.

88 **spernens**: Hannibal's contempt for the Gauls in this encounter led him never to put too much reliance on them later when they were his allies against Rome. There is a hint in the Latin that, while the Romans made heavy weather of the **Gallicos tumultus** (which could mean 'the turbulent Gauls'), Hannibal easily managed to cut them down to size.

Chapter 28 of Book 21 contains a memorable account of the crossing of the elephants. It would be worthwhile reading this to your pupils in translation (e.g. Aubrey de Sélincourt's, Penguin).

Illustrations

p. 168: this bust of Hannibal is in the National Archaeological Museum, Naples.

p. 169: the ruins of Carthage are not from the Phoenician city, which was almost completely obliterated by the Romans in 146 BC, but from a new town founded on the site by Augustus.

p. 172: in the foreground of this picture of Saguntum is the Roman theatre (built later, under Tiberius). The citadel dominates the site.

2 Hannibal reaches the Alps

Book 21.32.6–35.3

2–6 tum ex propinquo ...: this is one of those passages where Livy shows his unsurpassed historical empathy. He enters into the minds of the Carthaginians as they gaze in appalled terror at the sight which confronts them. Do your students feel that this should be thought of as imaginative writing, or could one apply to Livy here Hobbes' remark on Thucydides, that he did not 'enter into men's hearts further than the acts themselves guide him'? This was the situation; this *must* have been the reaction.

7ff. erigentibus ...: this episode may have taken place in the Col de Grimone.

19–20 pluribus ... factis: Hannibal is trying to give the impression that the whole army is in the camp. Thus the enemy will not suspect the existence of a storming party.

25ff. iam montani ...: the changing reactions of the Gauls are vividly conveyed.

53 populum: might mean 'region' or 'district' here.

54 suis artibus, fraude et insidiis: *Punica fides* was an ironical expression referring to the proverbial treachery of the Carthaginians. Again Roman prejudice makes itself felt.

66 in angustiorem viam: Hannibal may now be in the gorge of the River Guil.

Illustrations

p. 177: a scene of brutal fighting from Trajan's Column. Note how the Roman auxiliary soldier is carrying a barbarian's decapitated head in his teeth. 'He holds his short Roman sword, designed for thrusting rather than slashing, ready in his right hand as he meets the eyes of a Dacian (bottom right) ... At the left a German fighting on the Roman side, naked to the waist, lunges forward. He has a sword or dagger on his left side but prefers to use a club. These irregular troops kept their native methods of fighting' (R. L. Dalladay).

p. 180: a Carthaginian silver coin from Hannibal's time showing an African elephant. Comparing the size of the driver with the animal, one can see how small the African elephant was. (British Museum, London)

3 Hannibal crosses the Alps

Book 21.35.4–38.1, 39.51, Juvenal 10.147–67 (with one line omitted)

1–3 nono die ... faciebant: it looks as if Hannibal was simply hoping for the best in his search for a pass over the Alps.

7ff. fessis taedio tot malorum ...: another poignant passage in which Livy shows his empathy in his narrative.

10 promuntorio: this may have been near the Col de la Traversette, which is almost 10,000 feet high. John Ball wrote of this col: 'The view suddenly unfolded at the summit, extending in clear weather across the entire plain of Piedmont as far as Milan, is extremely striking.'

15 in manu ac potestate: a legal expression, suggesting Hannibal's belief that he and his men will soon be the lawful masters of Italy and Rome. Note the movement in this paragraph from abject despair to superb self-confidence.

16 ne ... quidem is mystifying. It seems to be there to contrast with **ceterum** (1. 17). The enemy did not bother them, but the terrain did.

pp. 182–3: this is an exciting but difficult passage in the Latin. We have therefore translated it.

32ff. inde ad rupem muniendam ...: this story has been ridiculed by many writers, but there is no reason to doubt it. De Beer cites a successful experiment by the Director of the British Museum in 1956. 'Blocks of limestone were covered with logs and were kindled into a hot fire, after which cold water containing ten per cent of acetic acid was thrown on to the stones. There was a cloud of steam and much hissing as the acid attacked the limestone, and when the cloud had cleared the limestone blocks were found to have been split.' De Beer concludes with a neat rebuke to the doubters: 'It is never safe to doubt factual statements of a practical nature by serious classical authors.'

40–41 iumentis ... absumptis: the elephants suffered particularly from the lack of food.

45–6 locis mollioribus et accolarum ingeniis: literally, 'the places (being) softer, i.e. easier to traverse, and the natures of the inhabitants (being softer, i.e. gentler)'.

47 hoc maxime modo ...: Hannibal got across with 12,000 African infantry, 8,000 Spaniards and all of the 37 elephants. He told a Roman prisoner that he had lost 36,000 men since crossing the Rhône.

48 T. = Titus. Explain that Roman names are usually given in full in translation.

65–7 liberemus ... censent: cf. Thomas North's translation of Plutarch: 'Titus Livius, that famous Historiographer, writeth, that Annibal called for the poyson he had ready for such a mischiefe, and that holding this deadly drinke in his hand, before he dranke he sayd: Come on, let us rid the Romans of this payne and care, sith their spight and malice is so great, to hasten the death of a poore old man that is halfe dead already.'

70–71 hic vitae exitus: Hannibal died when he was sixty-four. He was cornered, in the words of Plutarch, 'like a bird which had grown too old to fly and had lost its tail feathers'.

Juvenal: *Satires* 10.147ff.

4 Hispania, Pyrenaeum: as we have seen, Hannibal commanded the Carthaginian troops in Spain from 221 BC; he crossed the Pyrenees and then the Alps in 218 BC.

5 transilit: a striking use of enjambement (cf. **anulus** (1. 19)). Hannibal could move as swiftly as Alexander or Caesar.

8 actum ... nil est: Lucan wrote of Caesar, *nil actum credens cum quid superesset agendum* ('believing that nothing had been done when anything remained to be done').

19 anulus: it was particularly appropriate that the poison from a ring should take vengeance for Cannae. The messenger who took the news of the battle to Carthage confirmed his story by pouring out before the senators a vast heap of gold rings taken from the hands of the Roman knights who had been killed.

Samuel Johnson (1709–84) wrote a famous version of Juvenal's tenth satire, adapting it to the career of Charles XII of Sweden (*The Vanity of Human Wishes* 191–222):

> On what foundation stands the warrior's pride,
> How just his hopes let Swedish Charles decide;
> A frame of adamant, a soul of fire,
> No dangers fright him, and no labours tire;
> O'er love, o'er fear extends his wide domain,
> Unconquer'd lord of pleasure and of pain;
> No joys to him pacific scepters yield,
> War sounds the trump, he rushes to the field;
> Behold surrounding kings their pow'r combine,
> And one capitulate, and one resign;
> Peace courts his hand, but spreads her charms in vain;
> 'Think nothing gain'd,' he cries, 'till nought remain,
> On Moscow's walls till Gothic standards fly,
> And all be mine beneath the polar sky.'
> The march begins in military state,
> And nations on his eye suspended wait;
> Stern famine guards the solitary coast,

> And winter barricades the realms of Frost;
> He comes, not want and cold his course delay;
> Hide, blushing glory, hide Pultowa's* day:
> The vanquished hero leaves his distant bands,
> And shews his miseries in distant lands;
> Condemn'd a needy supplicant to wait,
> While ladies interpose, and slaves debate.
> But did not Chance at length her error mend?
> Did no subverted empire mark his end?
> Did rival monarchs give the fatal wound?
> Or hostile millions press him to the ground?
> His fall was destin'd to a barren strand,
> A petty fortress, and a dubious hand;
> He left the name, at which the world grew pale,
> To point a moral, or adorn a tale.

* Charles was defeated at the Battle of Pultowa (1709) after which he spent five years in Turkey, finally meeting his death by a sniper's bullet in 1718.

Some questions for your students: Is Johnson's adaptation more or less scornful than the original? Discuss the lasting relevance of the poets' theme. Do you take an equally jaundiced view of the achievements of great generals?

Look up details of Napoleon's crossing of the Alps in 1800. In Jacques-Louis David's great picture *Napoleon Crossing the St Bernard Pass*, Hannibal's name is carved on a rock.

Illustrations

p. 183: this equestrian statue of Marcus Balbus dates from the first centuries BC or AD. (National Archaeological Museum, Naples)

p. 185: Monte Viso is, at 3,841 m, the highest peak of the Cottian Alps. It looms over the Col de la Traversette, by which Hannibal may have crossed.

p. 188 (above): this bronze steelyard balance is from Pompeii. The fulcrum is eccentric; the scale pan hangs from the shorter arm and the counterweight (a general's head) hangs from a loop which is free to move along a graduated scale on the longer arm of the fulcrum. (National Archaeological Museum, Naples)

(below): this relief of an elephant is from a sarcophagus dating from c. AD 130–50. Bacchic revellers ride on top of the elephant. (Fitzwilliam Museum, Cambridge)

Ovid

The *Amores* and the *Ars Amatoria* are to be found in E. J. Kenney's Oxford Classical Text of Ovid's love poetry. *Amores* 1 has been edited by John Barsby, Oxford, repr. Bristol Classical Press, and *Ars Amatoria* 1 and *Metamorphoses* 8 by A. S. Hollis, Oxford. For English-speaking readers, the *Tristia* are available only in the Loeb edition (A. L. Wheeler, Heinemann).

All the love poetry and the poems from exile have been translated by A. D. Melville in the World's Classics series, Oxford (with admirable introductions and notes by E. J. Kenney), and by Peter Green in two valuable Penguin Classics (*Ovid: The Erotic Poems* and *Ovid: The Poems of Exile*). Guy Lee's translation of the *Amores* (John Murray) is highly recommended. The following books on Ovid are useful:

J. Barsby: *Ovid* (Greece & Rome New Surveys in the Classics), Oxford
J. W. Binns, ed.: *Ovid*, Routledge & Kegan Paul
E. J. Kenney: 'Ovid', in *The Cambridge History of Classical Literature*, vol. 2, ed. E. J. Kenney and W. V. Clausen, Cambridge, pp. 420–57 = *The Age of Augustus*, Cambridge, pp. 136–63
S. Mack: *Ovid*, Yale University Press
R. Syme: *History in Ovid*, Oxford
J. C. Thibaut: *The Mystery of Ovid's Exile*, University of California Press
L. P. Wilkinson: *Ovid Recalled*, Cambridge
G. Williams: *Banished Voices: Readings in Ovid's Exile Poetry*, Cambridge

1 Ovid tells the story of his life

Tristia 4.10.1–6, 9–12, 15–42, 45–6, 49–52, 55–60, 65–8, 93–4, 97–8; 1.3.1–22, 79–82, 85–9

1 **tenerorum lusor amorum**: Ovid draws attention both to the tenderness and to the playfulness of his love poetry.
2 **noris (= noveris)**: perfect subjunctive in a purpose clause. The perfect subjunctive is used instead of present since, while **nosco** = 'I get to know', **novi** (perfect) = 'I know'.
3 **Sulmo**: Ovid's love for the place of his birth is evident in his poetry, where its lushness and fertility are expressively conveyed. Modern Sulmona repays the compliment. Its official documents are headed with the initials SMPE (**Sulmo mihi patria est**) on the analogy of SPQR at Rome.
4 **novies ... decem**: the distance is in fact 94 Roman miles or 86 English miles.
8 **tribus ... quater**: Ovid's roundabout way with

numbers is partly due to the requirements of metre. It is impossible to use **duodecim** in Latin verse.
9 **Lucifer**: the light-bringer, i.e. the morning star.
12 **insignes ... viros**: it is not impossible that, when Ovid and his brother came to Rome in about 31 BC, they were taught by Horace's teacher, the *grammaticus* Orbilius. Ovid's teachers of rhetoric were Arellius Fuscus and Porcius Latro. The boys' father wanted to give both of them the education needed for the practice of law. This, he hoped, would prove the basis for successful political careers.
16 **Musa**: cf. 1. 46. The nine Muses were born in Pieria at the foot of Mount Olympus and dwelt on Mount Helicon in Boeotia. Cf. Michael Drayton (1562–1631) on Ben Jonson:

> Next these, learn'd Jonson, in this list I bring,
> Who had drunk deep of the Pierian spring.

18 **Maeonides**: Maeonia is the western district of Asia Minor where tradition maintains that Homer was born.
21–2 **sponte sua ...**: there is a story that Ovid's father rebuked him as a boy for scribbling poetry instead of doing his homework. The boy cried, *Parce mihi! nunquam versificabo, pater!* ('Forgive me, father! I'll never write a verse!'). This is a complete pentameter. (The **-o** at the end of **versificabo** scans short.) Pope's imitation of ll. 21–2 is famous (*Epistle to Dr Arbuthnot* 127–8):

> As yet a child, nor yet a fool to fame,
> I lisped in numbers, for the numbers came.

25 **cum lato purpura clavo**: the *equites illustres* (who had a capital reserve of at least 400,000 sesterces – the minimum required for entry to the senate) could wear two broad purple stripes on their toga. Other *equites* wore a narrow purple stripe and a golden ring. Augustus himself may have wished to support the political advancement of Ovid's family. See R. Syme: *The Roman Revolution*, Oxford, pp. 358–9.
28 **perit**: historic present, conveying an immediacy of feeling – especially after the elegant circumlocution of the previous line.
29–30 **cepimus ...**: he could not take the first step of a senatorial career until the age of thirty (when he could assume the quaestorship).
31 **curia**: i.e. a senatorial career.
36 **otia**: Ovid does not mean that he did nothing. He was in fact a highly productive poet. He is referring to a life removed from public affairs. **otium** frequently has this meaning.
39: Propertius (c. 50–c. 16 BC) addressed his love poetry to a woman whom he calls Cynthia.
41 **et tenuit ... aures**: this line could mean either that Ovid heard Horace recite, or that Horace's poetry charmed his ear, or both.

numerosus: as we have seen in Part III, Horace (65–8 BC) made use of many metres in his *Odes*. No major Latin poet chose to follow in Horace's footsteps in his use of Greek lyric metres.

42 culta: the word means something like 'elegant' or 'polished'. Augustan poets were not warblers of 'native wood-notes wild'. They aimed at a highly wrought sophistication.

43: Virgil (70–19 BC); Tibullus (55/48–19 BC).

47 carmina ... legi: for public recitals of poetry, see Pliny: *Letter* 47: 'This year has produced a great crop of poets; throughout the month of April there has scarcely been a day when nobody has given a recital. I am delighted that literature is flourishing and that so many talented men are coming forward to display their art; but the audience response is depressingly unenthusiastic. Most people sit in the porticos outside and while away the time they should be spending listening in idle chatter ... At long last – and even then slowly and reluctantly – they go in, but they do not stay to the end; they go out before then, some of them slipping away inconspicuously, but others leaving quite brazenly.'

50 nomine non vero: poets would choose a 'poetic' name for the object of their passion; it would be of the same metrical quantity as the real name (thus Clodia = Lesbia).

54 fabula nulla: Ovid claims elsewhere (*Tristia* 2.353–4) that, while his poetry was risqué, his life was pure:

> crede mihi, mores distant a carmine nostro –
> vita vercunda est, Musa iocosa mea.

> Believe me, my way of life is different from my poetry – my life is chaste, my Muse playful.

57–8 cum maris Euxini ...: Ovid was on Elba when the news of his banishment came. He was not in fact condemned to *exsilium* but to the less severe sentence of *relegatio*. This allowed him to keep his property and rights as a citizen. From Elba he went to Rome to prepare for his departure.

59–88: L. P. Wilkinson writes of the poem from which these lines are taken, 'It is a sincere and vivid record of a poignant personal experience, a thing rare in ancient poetry, except on the subject of love or death, though Cicero's Letters offer us counterparts in prose.'

69 Iovis ignibus: Jupiter wielded the thunderbolt (which combined thunder and lightning).

75 uxor: this was Ovid's third wife. His daughter was the child of his second wife. We do not know her name.

86 pietas: i.e. her dutiful love of her husband is as imperious as Caesar in its demands.

88 utilitate: his wife would be most useful if she stayed behind in Rome and fought for his interests there.

Illustrations

p. 190: The town of Sulmo had resisted Hannibal in 211 BC and supported Caesar in 49 BC. There was an important terraced sanctuary of Hercules Curinus outside the town.

p. 191: a statue put up in honour of Ovid in his home town in the Renaissance. Garlanded with the poet's crown of bays, he holds a book with the initials S.M.P.E. (*Sulmo mihi patria est*, p. 192, l. 3).

p. 193: this mosaic floor from a villa at Trier dates from the second century AD and shows the nine Muses. Top row: Thalia, muse of comedy, wreathed with ivy and holding a shepherd's crook and a comic mask; Terpsichore, muse of the dance, with a lyre; Clio, muse of history, with a scroll; middle row: Euterpe, muse of lyric poetry; an unidentified muse; Erato, muse of love poetry, holding a lyre; bottom row: Urania, muse of astronomy, with a celestial globe; two unidentified muses. The unidentified ones must be Calliope (epic), Melpomene (tragedy) and Polymnia (sacred song). (Rheinisches Landesmuseum, Trier)

p. 194: this statue of a togaed boy dates from the first century AD. (Vatican Museums, Rome)

p. 195: this contorniate portrait of Horace dates from the fourth century AD. (British Museum, London)

p. 196: Cupid is here shown sleeping on the lion skin of Hercules with the hero's club beside him. A lizard approaches his feet. The marble statue dates from the second century AD and may have decorated a child's tomb. It was found near the Porta Flaminia in Rome. (British Museum, London)

p. 198: Augustus is here represented as a pious citizen performing a sacrifice or attending a religious ceremony, with part of his toga drawn up to veil his head. (Museo delle Terme, Rome)

2 Ovid the lover

Amores 2.6.1–4, 11–14, 17–20, 37–8, 45, 48; *Amores* 1.5 (omitting ll. 11–12); *Ars Amatoria* 1.89–102, 107–10, 113–24, 127–32; *Amores* 3.2.1–14, 19–24, 65–84; *Metamorphoses* 8.618–22, 624–39, 679–94

Amores 2.6

The poem is a parody of the commemorative dirge. First the mourners are addressed (1–6), then there is the lamentation (7–14), followed by an account of the bird's death (15–16). There were good precedents for poems commemorating a dead pet. The most famous is Catullus 3 (see p. 116).

The humour implicit in the personification of the birds is beautifully handled. A talking bird is, of course, an especially apt candidate for such treatment. Corinna's parrot is a very special bird, an exotic pet, a lover's gift and a loving creature. Is there a measure of genuine pathos alongside the humour?

3–4 plangite pectora ...: at a Roman funeral, professional female mourners were hired to pull out their hair, beat their breasts and tear their cheeks with their fingernails.

Amores 1.5

This is the first poem in Latin literature simply describing love-making. It is in no way a prurient piece. The mood is one of relaxed hedonism.

19 pars adaperta ...: the windows are wooden shutters with transverse slats; one shutter is open.

23 verecundis: the girl who arrives is hardly shy!

ecce: 'the suddenness of her appearance suggests something superhuman ... [the middle of the day was] when the gods were apt to be abroad' (Kenney).

Ars Amatoria 1.89ff.

41 theatris: Ovid frequently refers to the theatre as a promising location for meeting girls.

45–8 ut ... formica ...: the similes of the ant and bees are taken from Virgil (see pp. 160 and 146). The use of similes from high (and patriotic) epic in such a context calls for discussion. Their Virgilian echoes apart, these are characteristically Ovidian similes, playful and not a little absurd as the humble insects are called upon to evoke the rush of the female *beau monde* (**cultissima femina**, 1. 49) to the theatre.

As the poem progresses, you may like to discuss with your pupils whether it is right to view it as subversive of Augustan values.

51–2 spectatum veniunt ...: Dryden wittily translates:

To see, and to be seen, in Heaps they run;
Some to undo, and some to be undone.

53ff. primus sollicitos ...: Ovid in this passage satirizes the aetiological tendency of Hellenistic poetry (i.e. its proneness to go back to the causes of things); and he pokes fun at the way in which Augustan literature makes use of early Roman legend to add grandeur and dignity to the nation's heritage (see especially Livy 1.9 and Virgil: *Aeneid* 8.635–6). Augustus had at one time considered adopting the name of Romulus, as the second founder of Rome. It is an amusingly impudent idea to present him as the patron of pick ups.

55–6 in gradibus ...: Ovid stresses the primitive conditions of the theatre in the early days of Rome. The seats were not of marble and there were no awnings stretched over the top, as there were in the Theatre of

Pompey in his time. Augustus claimed that he had found Rome brick and left it marble; but he would not have altogether appreciated Ovid's oblique tribute to Augustan theatres, with its implication that splendid surroundings are the perfect location for seduction.

57 respiciunt: in 18 BC Augustus had legislated that women should occupy only the back rows in the theatre. He aimed to keep the sexes apart. Ovid hints at the ineffectiveness of such legislation.

71 si qua repugnarat nimium: 'a notion which recurs time and again in the love-poets. It was right and proper for the girls to put up a show of reluctance, but not to carry their opposition too far' (Hollis).

75–6 Romule ...: the return to Romulus is a good example of a standard narrative technique, i.e. ring-composition (it was Romulus who started it all – this is how it happened – how splendid of Romulus!). The joke on **commoda** is precisely the sort of crack that may have got under Augustus' skin and contributed to Ovid's downfall. Augustus did in fact have difficulty in making the terms of service in the Roman army attractive. In effect Ovid is saying, 'If they could offer a pretty girl as a side-attraction nowadays, that would solve the recruiting problem' (Hollis). Dryden translates:

Thus *Romulus* became so popular;
This was the Way to thrive in Peace and War;
To pay his Army, and fresh Whores to bring;
Who wou'd not fight for such a gracious King!

Amores 3.2

Ovid is at the races in the stadium of the Circus Maximus in Rome. This huge rectangle with semicircular ends was surrounded by tiers of covered seats which held 250,000 spectators.

79 tecumque sederem: the sexes were kept apart at the theatre, but not at the Circus.

85 carcere: modern equivalents of *carceres* can be seen on today's race-courses; the *carcer* is *sacer* because it is a kind of gateway and all gateways and the like belonged to the god Janus. The chariots rushed from the starting boxes, beginning anticlockwise on the first of what were usually seven laps of the 550 metre track. They dashed along the right on a central division (*spina*, 'backbone') in the stadium. Each time a lap was finished, an object made of marble, either in the shape of an egg or a dolphin, was removed from the *spina*.

86 vehendus: the gerundive of **vehor** ('I ride') expresses purpose ('so as to ride') but in fact suggests little more than a future participle; 'riding' seems to us the less cumbersome translation.

105–6 sed enim revocate ...: races could in fact be stopped and re-started in the manner described here.

After reading these poems set at the theatre and the races, it may be profitable to discuss with your pupils why Ovid has chosen the background of entertainment and sport for his love poetry.

110 **discolor**: 'Circus factions in the later Empire throw modern football hooliganism into the shade' (Kenney). See A. Cameron: *Circus Factions: Blues and Greens at Rome and Byzantium*, Oxford.

Metamorphoses 8.618ff.

No telling of this story exists in Latin literature before Ovid. However, the theme of a god or a great figure entering a humble house was a popular one. In *Aeneid* 8, for example, Evander invites Aeneas to follow the example of the demigod Hercules and stoop to enter his simple dwelling (364–5).

The range of feeling and tone in the *Metamorphoses* is vast. In this episode, Baucis (the wife) and Philemon (the husband) show an ideal simplicity, looking back to Rome's rustic beginnings (cf. Horace's story of the town and country mouse (*Satires* 2.6.79–117)). There is little of Virgil's intensity or depth of emotion. But Ovid, deftly combining lightness of touch with an underlying seriousness, creates an episode in which we willingly suspend our disbelief. No poet, except for Homer in the *Odyssey*, has brought the miraculous into the real world more convincingly.

Ovid conveys the key Augustan virtue of *pietas* with panache and humour. The contrast with the grave profundity of Virgil's treatment of the same concept is fascinating. Ovid's use of detail is particularly effective. 'I see *Baucis* and *Philemon* as perfectly before me,' wrote Dryden, 'as if some ancient Painter had drawn them.'

124 **specie mortali**: Zeus (Jupiter) and Hermes (Mercury) were jointly worshipped in Asia Minor. Cf. Acts of the Apostles 14:11–12: 'And when the people saw what Paul had done, they lifted up their voices, saying in the speech of Lycaonia, "The gods are come down to us in the likeness of men." And they called Barnabas, Jupiter, and Paul Mercurius, because he was the chief speaker.'

143–7 **unicus anser erat ...**: here is Dryden's version of part of this passage:

> One Goose they had ('twas all they cou'd allow)
> A wakeful Cent'ry, and on Duty now,
> Whom to the Gods for Sacrifice they vow:
> Her, with malicious Zeal, the Couple view'd;
> She ran for Life, and limping they pursu'd:
> Full well the Fowl perceiv'd their bad intent,
> And wou'd not make her Masters Compliment;
> But persecuted, to the Pow'rs she flies,
> And close between the Legs of *Jove* she lies:

> He with a gracious Ear the Suppliant heard,
> And sav'd her Life.

145–7 **ille celer ...**: 'Their vain attempts to catch the goose make a contrast with the unhurried and dignified gods, and also prevent the narrative from becoming too elevated' (Hollis). The goose, as Dryden perceives, becomes a suppliant, running to the gods to beg their assistance. Supplication was a serious business in the ancient world, and the god or human who was called upon for help would feel a certain obligation to give it. The gods do so here.

Illustrations

p. 200 (above): this mosaic is from Pompeii. It dates from the first century AD. (National Archaeological Museum, Naples)

(below): this superb statue of Parian marble is a Roman replica of a Hellenistic original, derived from the Cnidian Aphrodite of Praxiteles (third quarter of the fourth century BC) which was supposedly modelled on his mistress Phryne: this was the first completely naked female Greek statue. Venus has been surprised while about to bathe and has covered herself with instinctive modesty. Of the reconstructed Praxiteles, Susan Woodford says, 'The limp, inert drapery and the rigid water-jar contrast with the soft, living body of the goddess.' Our statue was found in the seventeenth century in a house near San Vitale, Rome, and is called the Capitoline Venus because it stands in the Capitoline Museum in Rome.

p. 201: this mosaic of doves drinking from a bowl, a popular subject, is from Hadrian's villa at Tivoli (second century AD). It is probably a Roman copy of an original by Sosias of Pergamon. (Capitoline Museum, Rome)

p. 202: the theatre at Orange in Provence in the south of France dates from the first century AD. The massive back wall of the stage, with its turret-like projections, was originally decorated elaborately with marble architecture.

p. 204: this relief portraying the rape of the Sabine women was put on the Basilica Aemilia in the Forum on its restoration, financed by Augustus, probably in 14 BC.

p. 207: the Circus Maximus lay in the Vallis Murcia between the Palatine and Aventine hills. The vast model, of which this photo shows a small part, is in the Museo della Civiltà Romana, Rome.

p. 208: this terracotta relief made in Italy in the first century AD shows a chariot race. A four-horsed chariot approaches the turning-post with its three decorated columns. The driver reins in his horses. A *jubilator*, a rider who encourages the contestants, has just turned. By the turning post, there crouches – just visible – a fallen charioteer. (British Museum, London)

p. 210: the shrine (at the top) takes the form of a little temple with Corinthian columns. It contains statues of the household gods. The cupboard contains glassware and ornaments. From the House of the Wooden Shrine at Herculaneum.

p. 211: this statue of a child playing with a goose is a Roman copy of a Hellenistic composition of the third century BC. (Louvre Museum, Paris)

3 Ovid in exile

Tristia 1.2.1–2, 19–26, 31–4; 3.10.1–10, 13–14, 17–22, 25–6, 31–2, 37–8, 47–50, 53–8, 61–70, 75–8; 3.3.1–4, 7–18; 5.7.39–46, 51–6; *Amores* 3.9.1–6, 35–40, 59–62, 65–8

Tristia 1.2, 3.10, 3.3, 5.7

The Emperor had insisted that Ovid depart in mid-winter, thus increasing the likelihood of a stormy voyage. Tomis, now Costantza in Romania, is near the mouth of the Danube. In modern times, Costantza is a popular holiday resort for Eastern Europeans with a temperature ranging from 80°F (27°C) in the summer to 25°F (-4°C) in the winter. Inland, however, it sometimes drops to -20°F (-29°C) or more.

One result of Ovid's banishment was that this famous love poet totally lost interest in sex (*ex Ponto* 4.2.33–4).

1ff. **di maris et caeli ...:** *Tristia* Book 1, Ovid claims (*Tristia* 1. 11), was at least in part written during his voyage to Tomis. The storm described here, therefore, may be a real one, but the hyperbolical description makes it 'a metaphor for his own fate' (Kenney).

6 **Tartara:** Tartarus was the place of punishment in the underworld. Hesiod writes that it is as far below the earth as heaven is above.

8 **hic ... ille:** 'the latter ... the former'. Explain this usage to your students: **hic** ('this') means 'the latter' because of the two items previously mentioned it refers to the one closer to it.

21 **Histro:** Hister usually refers to the lower part of the Danube.

37 **pontum:** *pontus* means 'sea'; but it can refer specifically to the Black Sea.

87–8 **in paucis ...:** barbarians are those who cannot speak Greek (they say 'barbar'). In fact, as Ovid says, a debased Greek was spoken in the area.

90 **e medio ... verba:** words in common use as opposed to literary or educated language.

Elsewhere Ovid complains that writing poetry which he can read to nobody is like dancing in the dark.

'If you put Homer himself in this land, believe me, he would become a Getan' (*ex Ponto* 4.2.33–4, 21–2).

Ovid learnt the local languages and received kind treatment from the people of Tomis, who exempted him from taxes. A statue of Ovid stands in the main square of Constantza (see illustration on p. 214).

Amores 3.9

Ovid's fellow-poet Tibullus wrote about love and the countryside. His elegiac couplets are plain but polished. He is never strident but conveys the depth of his feelings with a quiet intensity. We cannot be sure how old Tibullus was when he died in 19 BC (in the same year as Virgil). Ovid later referred to him as dying young:

> te quoque Vergilio comitem non aequa, Tibulle,
> mors iuvenem campos misit ad Elysios.

> Unjust death sent you also, Tibullus, as a companion to Virgil to the Elysian fields while you were still young.

This poem is a funeral lament (compare and contrast the elegy for Corinna's parrot, p. 200). The chief mourner is addressed (91–6); there follow the lament (97–102), the *consolatio* (103–8) and a brief *requiem* in conclusion.

There is dignity and sincere emotion in this poem, as well as a high seriousness in its tragic vision of a world where death seems at first to be the only reality. But the *consolatio*, with its delightful evocation of a poets' heaven, movingly asserts the victory of poetry over death and leads to the poignant diminuendo of the concluding prayer.

The fine simplicity of these lines recalls Catullus' lament for his brother (pp. 130–31).

93 **Elegeia:** the word 'elegy' is more likely to be connected with some foreign word meaning a flute – so that an elegy is a flute song. Early elegies are in fact not usually laments.

103–8 **si tamen ...:** this beautifully poised passage no doubt owes something to Socrates' speculations about death at the end of Plato's *Apology*. It inspired Thomas Dekker to set a fraternity of dead Elizabethan writers in the Elysian fields (1607):

> Marlowe, Greene, and Peele had got under the shade of a large vine, laughing to see Nashe (that was but new come to their college) still haunted with the sharp and satirical spirit that followed him here on earth.

16 **docte:** in our Catullus chapters, we have

concentrated on his more passionate and direct poetry. Nevertheless we hope that his dedication to his craft as a poet – and his mastery of it – will have come across. He is one of the most technically proficient of Latin poets.

18 **culte**: see n. on 1. 42 in ch. 1 (p. 45 above).

Illustrations

p. 216: a Scythian bronze dating from about 500 BC. Cf. the illustration on p. 128, and note (p. 33 above). (British Museum, London)
p. 218: this mummy-portrait of a woman from Antinoopolis in Roman Egypt dates from the first half of the second century AD. (Louvre Museum, Paris)
p. 220: in this relief of a funeral from a Roman sarcophagus of the first century BC or AD, musicians lead the way; the dead man reclines as if he is observing his own funeral, the pall with its decoration of moon and stars unrealistically raised; his family follow behind. (Museo Aquilano, Aquilla, Abruzzi).
p. 221: this glass urn, containing the ashes of a cremated body, dates from the first or second century AD. (Harrow School).

Translations

Cicero

1 The young Cicero

de Legibus 2.1.2–3

Atticus: I used to be surprised, thinking that there was nothing but rocks and mountains in this district, that you took such great delight in this place; now, on the contrary, I'm surprised that when you are away from Rome, there's anywhere you'd rather be.

Cicero: Certainly, when I can be away from Rome for a few days, especially at this time of year, I make for the beauty and healthy climate here; yet I rarely have the chance. But in fact there's another reason it delights me, which does not extend to you, Titus.

Atticus: Whatever is that reason?

Cicero: It's because, to tell the truth, this is the true native country of myself and my brother here; for here we were born, sprung from a very ancient stock; here are our private rites, here our family, here the traces of our ancestors. In short, you see this house, as it now is, built more grandly by the efforts of our father, who because he was of weak health, pretty well spent his life here in literature, but in this very place, when my grandfather was alive and the house was small in the old fashion, I was born. And so there is something hidden deep in the feelings of my mind, because of which, perhaps, this place gives me an extra pleasure, seeing that the wisest of men (Odysseus) is said to have rejected immortality in order to see Ithaca (again).

Brutus 306

But I gave much attention to Quintus Scaevola in my study of civil law, who although he never offered formal teaching to anyone, used to teach those keen to listen by his replies to the clients who consulted him.

And at the same time, when Philo, the head of the Academy, fled from home in the Mithridatic war together with the leading men of Athens and came to Rome, I devoted myself to him completely, stirred on by an extraordinary enthusiasm for philosophy; and I concentrated on this even more attentively for this reason, that the whole system of legal practice now seemed to have been destroyed for good. Sulpicius had died that year and the next year three orators were most cruelly put to death, Q. Catulus, M. Antonius, C. Julius. The same year I also studied under Molon in Rome, a first-class advocate (pleader of cases) and teacher.

pro Plancio 65

I have no fears, gentlemen of the jury, that I may seem to boast if I speak of my quaestorship. For, however successful that may have been, I think that after it I have so conducted myself (have been such) in the highest offices, that I do not need to seek so much glory from praise of my quaestorship. However, I am not afraid that anyone would dare to say that any man's (tenure of the) quaestorship in Sicily was either more famous or more popular. By god, I will say this, and it's true: at that time I thought that people at Rome were talking about nothing but my quaestorship. I had sent a large quantity of corn (to Rome) when there was a great scarcity; I had been courteous to the business men, fair to the merchants, generous to the tax-farmers, honest in my dealings with our allies; everyone thought I had been extremely conscientious in (the performance of) every duty; indeed, honours unheard of had been devised for me by the Sicilians. And so I left hoping and believing (with this hope, that I thought) that the people of Rome would offer me everything without my asking.

But it happened at that time that as I was leaving my province to make a journey I came by chance to Puteoli at the time when a very large number of the smartest people are habitually (accustomed to be) in that district; I almost collapsed, gentlemen, when someone asked me on what day I had left Rome and whether there was any news. I answered him that I was retiring from my province. 'Yes, of course,' he said, 'from Africa, I believe.' I was annoyed and answered him disdainfully, 'No, from Sicily.' Then some know-all said, 'What? Don't you know? He has been quaestor at Syracuse.' In short, I stopped being annoyed and made myself one of the throng who had come to (take) the waters.

ad Atticum 1.5.2, 7–8

As for what you write about your sister, she herself will be witness of what trouble I have taken to make my brother Quintus feel towards her as he should. Since I thought he had been rather offensive towards her, I wrote a letter to him to placate him as my brother, to advise him as my junior, and to scold him for his faults. And so, judging from what he has often written to me since, I am confident that all is as it should be and as we would want.

I'm delighted that you are pleased with your purchase in Epirus. We are expecting Quintus (here) every day. Terentia has terrible pains in her joints. She has great affection for you and your sister and your mother and adds her heartiest greetings to you, and so does my darling little Tullia. See that you keep well and love us, and be assured (persuade yourself) that I love you like a brother.

ad Atticum 1.2

Cicero sends greetings to Atticus.

This is to tell you (know!) that I have been blessed with a little son, and Terentia is well.

No letter from you now for a long time! I wrote to you carefully earlier about my plans. At the moment I am thinking of defending Catiline, my fellow candidate. We have the jury we want with the full cooperation of the prosecutor. I hope, if he is acquitted, he will be more closely allied (with me) in our election campaign.

I need you to come here soon. For certainly people's general opinion is that your friends, the nobles, will oppose my election. I see that you will be very useful to me in winning their support. And so see that you are in Rome at the beginning of January, as you have decided.

2 Consulship, exile and return

in Catilinam 1.1

However long are you going to abuse our patience, Catiline? And how long will that madness of yours mock us? To what end will your unbridled audacity vaunt itself? Are you quite unmoved by the nightly guard on the Palatine, by the watches in the city, by the fear of the people, by the gatherings of all good men, by the expression on the faces of your fellow senators (these men)? Don't you realize that your schemes are revealed, that your conspiracy is now held fast, chained by the knowledge of all these men? Do you think that there is anyone who does not know what you did last night, what you did the night before, where you have been, with whom you met, what plans you have made?

O what (shocking) times, what behaviour! The senate knows this, the consul sees it; yet this man is still alive.

ad Familiares 5.7.2–3

I have no doubt of this, that if my hearty support for you has failed to bring us together, public interest will unite and join us to each other. And in case you do not know what I missed in your letter, I will write openly, as my nature and our friendship demands. I have done deeds for which I expected some congratulation in your letter both because of our close friendship and because of the political situation; and I suppose you omitted this because you were afraid you might offend someone's feelings. But you must be aware that what I did for the salvation of our country is heartily approved by the judgement and testimony of the whole world; when you come, you will learn that I did these things with such wisdom and such courage (greatness of mind) that you will gladly allow me, who am not much inferior to Laelius, to be united with you, who are much greater than Africanus, both in politics and in friendship.

ad Atticum 2.19.2–3

You must know that nothing has ever been so infamous, so disgraceful, so unpopular with all classes, ranks and ages alike as the present state of affairs. Bibulus is praised to the skies; why, I don't know, but he is praised as if

'One man alone has restored our fortunes by delaying'.

Pompey, my loved one, has ruined himself, which is very painful to me. He holds no one by goodwill; I am afraid they (the triumvirs) may have to use intimidation. The feeling of the people is most clearly seen in the theatre and at shows; at the games of Apollo the tragic actor Diphilus attacked our Pompey insolently:

'It's through our misery that you are Great —'

He was forced to say (this line) a thousand times. When Caesar arrived after the applause had died down, Curio junior followed him in. He was applauded as Pompey used to be when the republic was still unharmed. Caesar took it badly.

ad Atticum 3.19.3

I beg and beseech you, Titus Pomponius, if you see that I have been stripped of all the things I loved and enjoyed in such ample measure through the treachery of men, if you see that I have been betrayed and thrown over by my advisers, if you understand that I have been forced to ruin myself and my family, (then I beg you) in your compassion to help me and support my brother

Quintus, who can still be saved, to watch over Terentia and my children, to wait for me, if you think I shall see you in Italy, if not, to visit me (here), if you can, and to send me your slaves with letters as soon as you can and as often as you can. Dispatched 16 September.

ad Familiares 14.2.1–2, 4

Cicero sends greetings to his Terentia, his little Tullia and Cicero (junior).

Don't suppose that I write longer letters to anyone, except to anyone who has written to me at greater length who I think I should answer. For I have nothing to write and at this time there is nothing I find harder to do. I can't write to you and our little Tullia without floods of tears. For I see that you are utterly miserable, who I always wanted to be very happy, and I should have achieved this, and would have done so unless I had panicked.

I see that you are doing everything with the greatest courage and love, and I'm not surprised at this, but I grieve at a misfortune of such a kind that my unhappiness is lightened by such great unhappiness of your own. Ah, light of my life, my darling, from whom (where) everyone used to find strength, to think that you are so buffeted, that you lie so low in tears and squalor, and that this is happening through my fault – I saved others so that we should perish!

I don't know who to write to, except to those who write to me. Since that is what you want, I shall not go further away (from Italy); but I should like you to send letters as often as possible, especially if there is any firmer news about our hopes.

Goodbye, my darlings, goodbye. Dispatched 5 October, Thessalonica.

ad Atticum 4.1.4–5, 8

Although I think that by now you have had a written account of everything from your friends or that it has been reported to you by messages and rumour, I shall still write briefly what I think you would most like to learn from a letter from me.

On 4 August I set out from Dyrrachium, on the very day that the law was proposed about me. I arrived at Brundisium on 5 August. There was my little Tullia to meet me on her very birthday, which happened to be also the birthday of the colony of Brundisium; this was noticed by the crowd and celebrated with the enthusiastic congratulations of the people of Brundisium. On 11 August, while I was at Brundisium, I learnt through a letter from my brother Quintus that the law had been passed in the Centuriate assembly with wonderful enthusiasm of men of every age and class, and an incredible gathering of people from Italy. Then, loaded with honours from the people of Brundisium, I journeyed on with embassies coming together from everywhere to congratulate me (I made my journey in such a way that ...). I came to the city (Rome) in such style that there was no one of any rank known to my name-caller who failed to come to meet me. When I came to the Capena gate, the steps of the temples were filled with the common people; their congratulations were shown me by tremendous applause and similar throngs and applause greeted me right up to the Capitol, and in the Forum and on the Capitol itself there was an amazing crowd. The following day I offered thanks in the senate to the senate.

I am beginning a sort of start to a second life. Already some who defended me in my absence are starting to be secretly angry and openly jealous at the present state of affairs. I need you badly.

ad Atticum 4.3.2–3

On 3 November the workmen were driven from our building site by armed men, my brother Quintus' house was first smashed up by a hail of stones from our site, and then set alight on Clodius' orders as fire was thrown at it before the eyes of the whole city, with loud complaints and groans from everyone. Even before this Clodius was dashing about like a madman, but after this piece of lunacy he thinks of nothing but the murder of his enemies, he parades the streets (gathering support) and openly offers his slaves the hope of liberty.

On 11 November, when I was going down the Sacred Way, he pursued me with his gang. Shouting, stones, clubs, swords! and all of this out of the blue! I got away into the forecourt of Tettius Damon('s house). Those who were with me easily stopped the gangs from getting in. Clodius himself might have been killed; but I begin to practise cure by diet, I'm tired of surgery.

ad Quintum Fratrem 2.3.2

On 6 February Milo appeared in court. Pompey spoke, or rather he wanted to; for the moment he got up, Clodius' gangs raised a shout, and this continued throughout the whole of his speech, so that he was hampered not only by shouts of disapproval but also by insults and abuse. When he had ended his speech (for in this he was certainly brave; he was not deterred; he said everything and sometimes even in silence when he triumphed by his authority) – but when he had finished, up got Clodius. There was such a shout raised by our side (for we had decided to return the compliment) that he could not control his mind, tongue or face. This went on from when Pompey had scarcely finished his speech at the sixth hour, right up to the eighth hour, while every insult and finally the most obscene verses were hurled against Clodius and Clodia. Pale with rage (raging and bloodless) he asked his followers in the midst of the uproar who it was that was killing the people with hunger; his gangs replied 'Pompey'. At about the ninth hour as though at a given signal Clodius' gangs began to spit in unison; anger flared up. They shoved to move us from our place; our men charged them; the gangs fled; Clodius was thrown off the Rostra, and we too fled, in case anything should happen in the crush. The senate was summoned to the senate house; Pompey went home; and I did not go to the senate either.

ad Familiares 7.5

Cicero sends greetings to *imperator* Caesar.

See how I have convinced myself that you are my second self, not only in matters which concern myself but also in those which concern my friends. I send you Gaius Trebatius, of whom I make this guarantee, there is no more honest person, no man better, none more modest; besides this he leads the field in civil law, a man of uniquely good memory and the widest knowledge. I don't ask for him a tribunate or a prefecture or any particular piece of patronage; I hand the whole man over to you. See that you keep well and continue to be my friend (love me as you do).

ad Familiares 7.7

I continue to recommend you, but what progress I am making I want to know from you. I have the greatest hope in Balbus, to whom I write very carefully and very often. I often wonder at this, that I don't get letters from you as often as I do from my brother Quintus.

I hear there is no gold or silver in Britain. If that is so, I advise you to get hold of a war chariot and run back to us as soon as possible. But if we can achieve what we want without (your going to) Britain, see that you become one of Caesar's friends. My brother will help you a lot in this, Balbus will help a lot, but, believe me, it's your own modesty and industry that will help most. You have a most generous general, exactly the right age, and certainly a unique recommendation, so that you have only one thing to fear, that you may seem to have let yourself down.

ad Quintum Fratrem 2.15.4–5

I now come to what should perhaps have come first. Oh, how glad I was to get your letter from Britain! I was afraid of the Ocean, I was afraid of the island's shore; I certainly don't discount (despise) the rest, but that provides more hope than fear and I was more worried by that waiting for news than by actual fear. But I see that you have outstanding material for writing. What sites you have, what strange things and places, what customs, what peoples, what battles and, indeed, what a general!

What did Caesar think of my verses, brother? For he wrote to me earlier that he had read the first book and he so (enjoyed) the first part that he says he's never read anything better even in Greek.

3 Governor of Cilicia

ad Atticum 5.16

Cicero sends greetings to Atticus.

Although the publicans' letter-carriers are leaving in the middle of my journey and on the road and we are on the march, I still thought I must snatch a moment, so that you should not think that I have forgotten your instructions. And so I've sat down on the actual road while I write this account to you in brief.

Let me tell you (know!) that I arrived on 31 July amidst the greatest expectation at a province which has been ruined and turned upside down for ever. I have heard nothing but the groans and laments of the cities and the monstrous deeds not of a man but of some dreadful wild animal. What do you expect? They are completely tired of life. But the unhappy cities are relieved because no expense is made on me or on my legates or on my quaestor or on anyone at all (of my staff). And so people are gathering (gatherings are taking place) in a incredible way from the fields, the villages and all the towns; and all of them are coming to life again even at my mere arrival, when they learn of the justice, honesty and mercy of your Cicero.

Not a sound from the Parthian(s), but all the same we heard from people who come that our cavalry had been cut up by the barbarians. We are hurrying to our camp, which is two days' march away.

ad Atticum 5.20.2–3

I arrived at my camp on 26 August. I reviewed my army on the 30th at Iconium. I proceeded from this camp, since serious intelligence was coming in about the Parthians, into Cilicia through the part of

Cappadocia which borders on Cilicia, with the intention of making the Parthians think they were shut out of Cappadocia. When I had kept my camp near Cybistra in Cappadocia for five days, I was informed that the Parthians were far from this approach to Cappadocia and were rather threatening Cilicia. And so I marched at speed into Cilicia through the Gates of Taurus. I reached Tarsus on 5 October. From there I marched to Amanus, which divides Syria from Cilicia at the watershed; this mountain was full of permanent enemies. Here on 13 October I slew a large number of the enemy. I took some heavily fortified castles with a night attack from Pomptinus (with the arrival of Pomptinus at night), and one from myself in the morning. I was hailed *imperator*. For several days I kept the very same camp as Alexander had kept opposite Darius at Issus, a general considerably better than you or me. After staying for five days and plundering and laying waste Amanus, we left there. Meanwhile on the report of our arrival Cassius, who was held in Antioch, plucked up courage and at the same time the Parthians had a dose of fear.

ad Familiares 2.12

Marcus Cicero *imperator* sends greetings to Marcus Caelius curule aedile.

I am worried about affairs at Rome. Such turbulent public meetings, such a tiresome celebration of the festival of Minerva is reported here; for I've heard nothing yet of later events. But nothing upsets me more than that in these troubles I'm not laughing with you, if there is anything to be laughed at; for there is a great deal, but I don't dare to write about it. I am distressed that I've still had no letter from you about all this. And so, even if, by the time you read this, I shall have already completed my year's tour of duty, I would still like a letter from you to meet me, to inform me about the whole political situation, so that I don't arrive (at Rome) like an absolute foreigner. There is no one who can do this better than you.

Rome, Rufus, stick to Rome, and live in its light there! All foreign service, as I've judged from my youth, is obscure and mean for those whose industry can shine in Rome. Since I knew this very well, I wish I had stuck to this conviction! Good lord, I don't compare all the profits of a province with one little walk and one chat with you. But, I hope, I shall see you soon. Do (you) send a letter to meet me worthy of yourself.

ad Familiares 8.14.1–3

Caelius sends greetings to Cicero.

It was not worth capturing Arsace and storming

Seleucea to miss the spectacle of what has happened here; your eyes would never have been sore (again), if you had seen the face of Domitius at his rejection (at the polls). For that was an important election and support was plainly based on party feelings.

On the general political situation I have often written to you that I don't see peace lasting out the year, and the nearer that struggle comes, as come it must, the clearer the danger appears. The issue about which the power-mongers are going to fight is this, that Cn. Pompey has decided not to allow Caesar to become consul except on condition that he resigns his army and province, but Caesar is convinced that he can't be safe if he gives up his army; he makes this condition, that they should both resign their armies. So their love for one another and their hated alliance has not lapsed into secret bickering, but has burst out into war. In this struggle I see that Cn. Pompey will have the senate and the jury panel on his side, and that all who live in fear or ill hopes will go over to Caesar; their armies are not to be compared. In any case there is plenty of time to weigh up their forces and choose one's side.

ad Familiares 16.1

Tullius and his son Cicero and his brother and his brother's son send heartiest greetings to Tiro.

I thought I could bear my separation from you a little more easily, but plainly I can't and, although it is most important to the honour due to me that I arrive in Rome as soon as possible, I nevertheless feel that I have done wrong in leaving you; but because it seemed to be your wish that you absolutely refused to sail until you were better (except when your body was strengthened), I approved your decision and don't change my mind now, if you still feel the same; but if, after you have taken some food, you think you can catch me up, that's for you to decide. I have sent Mario to you, so that either he can come to me with you, or if you stay, he may return to me at once. But you can be sure of this, that if it can be done without harming your health, there is nothing I want more than that you should be with me; but if you know that you need to stay a little at Patrae to recover, there is nothing I want more than that you should be well. If you sail at once, you will catch us up at Leucas; but if you want to get stronger, take care (you will see carefully) that you have suitable companions, weather and ship. Dear Tiro, please (if you love me) remember (see) this one thing, that Mario's arrival and this letter must not influence you. And so above all see that you get well. Of all your innumerable services to me this is the most welcome.

4 Civil war and death

ad Atticum 9.6a

Caesar *imperator* sends greetings to Cicero *imperator*.

Although I had only just seen our friend Furnius and could not talk with him or listen to him at my convenience, since I was in haste and had already sent on my legions and was on the march, I could not omit to write to you and send him to you and thank you, although I have often done this (i.e. thanked you) and imagine I shall often do so again; that's what you deserve from me. Above all I ask, since I am confident I shall soon come near Rome, to see you there, so that I can make use of your advice, influence, importance and assistance in everything. You will forgive my haste and the shortness of my letter. You will learn everything else from Furnius.

ad Atticum 9.11a.1

Cicero *imperator* sends greetings to Caesar *imperator*.

When I read your letter which I have received from our friend Furnius, in which you tried to persuade me to meet you (to be) near Rome, I was not much surprised that you wanted to use 'my advice and importance'; but I asked myself what you meant by 'my influence' and 'help'; however, I was optimistically persuaded to think (I was led on by hope to this thought) that in view of your admirable and unique wisdom you wanted to have discussions about the tranquillity, peace and harmony of our citizens, and I thought my nature and character suitable enough for such a policy.

ad Familiares 14.7

Tullius sends heartiest greetings to his Terentia.

All the vexation and worries by which I made both you and little Tullia, who is dearer to me than my own life, most unhappy, I have given up and banished. I learnt the cause of them the day after I left you. In the night I vomited up a great deal of bile. I was at once so relieved that some god seemed to have given me a cure.

I hope we have a very good ship. As soon as I had boarded it, I wrote this. Next I shall write many letters to our friends, in which I shall commend you and our Tullia most carefully. I would be encouraging you to be braver at heart unless I knew that you are braver than any man. First I should like you to look after your health; then, if it seems right to you, use those villas which are furthest from soldiers. You will be able to make good use of our farm at Arpinum with our Roman household, if the price of food goes up.

Our handsome young Cicero sends you heartiest greetings. Again and again, farewell.

ad Familiares 14.20

Tullius sends greetings to his Terentia.

I think I shall come to our Tusculan villa on either the 7th or the next day. See that everything is ready there. For perhaps there will be several people with me and we shall, I think, stay there for some time. If there is no basin in the bathroom, see that there is; and similarly everything else which is necessary for subsistence and health. Goodbye.

ad Atticum 12.15

Cicero sends greetings to Atticus.

In this solitude I talk to no one, and when I have hidden myself in a thick and thorny wood early in the morning, I don't leave it before evening. Second to you there is nothing dearer to me than solitude. In this solitude my talk is entirely with literature. But tears interrupt it; I fight against them as far as I can, but I'm not yet up to it. I will reply to Brutus, as you advise. You will have the letter tomorrow.

ad Atticum 13.52

Cicero sends greetings to Atticus.

O, such an onerous guest, but I don't regret having had him. For he was very cheerful. But when he came to Philippus in the evening of the second day of the Saturnalia, the villa was so filled with soldiers that there was scarcely a dining-room free for Caesar himself to dine in; why, there were two thousand men. I was very worried about what would happen the next day; but Barba Cassius came to my rescue and provided guards. The (soldiers') camp was in the field; the villa was in a state of defence. On the third day of the Saturnalia he stayed with Philippus until the seventh hour and let no one in; doing accounts, I think, with Balbus. Then he took a walk on the beach. After the eighth hour he took a bath. He was anointed and took his place at table. He was having a course of emetics; and so he ate and drank cheerfully without worrying.

Besides (him) his retinue was entertained generously in three dining-rooms. There was plenty (nothing lacking) for his less grand freedmen and slaves. For I entertained the grander ones handsomely. In short I showed myself a man. But he is not the sort of guest to whom you would say, 'Please, visit me again on your way back.' Once is enough. There was nothing of importance in our conversation, a lot about literature. In short, he was delighted and cheerful. He said he would spend one day at Puteoli and a second at Baiae.

ad Familiares 6.15

Cicero sends greetings to Basilus.

I congratulate you, I'm delighted; I love you and watch over your interests; I want to know that I am loved by you and what you are doing and what your plans are.

ad Familiares 9.24.4

But don't, please, think that, because I write to you rather humorously, I have abandoned my care for the state. Let me assure you (persuade yourself of this), dear Paetus, that night and day I am pursuing nothing and caring about nothing, except that my fellow citizens should be safe and free. I omit no opportunity for giving advice, taking action, looking to the future; in fact what I feel is that if I risk my life in this conscientious management of affairs, I believe all is well with me. Again and again farewell.

Tusculan Disputations 1.117

Although this is so, we have to use great eloquence, so that men shall either begin to wish for death or at least stop fearing it. For if that last day does not bring annihilation but a change of place, what is more desirable? But if it destroys us utterly and completely, what is better than to fall asleep in the midst of the toils of life and so closing our eyes be lulled in everlasting sleep?

Livy: fragment 50

Marcus Cicero, certain, as was true, that he could not be rescued from Antony, first fled to his Tusculan villa, then set out for his villa at Formiae, intending to take a ship from Caieta. From there he sailed out to sea several times, but when sometimes contrary winds carried him back, sometimes he could not bear the tossing of the ship, he at last became weary of both flight and life. He returned to his villa inland (higher) and said, 'I shall die in the country I have often saved.' It is well known that his slaves were ready to fight fiercely and loyally; but he himself ordered the litter to be put down and (told them) to endure quietly what cruel fate was forcing. He held his neck out of the litter and kept it still as his head was cut off. Nor was this enough for the brutish cruelty of the soldiers; they cut off his hands too, reproaching them for having written things against Antony. So his head was brought back to Antony, and by his order was fixed between his two hands on the Rostra, where he had been listened to with admiration for his eloquence as consul, as ex-consul, and that very year speaking against Antony. People could scarcely raise their eyes for tears to look upon his mutilated limbs.

Caesar

1 The first invasion of Britain

de Bello Gallico 4.20–22

The campaign season was almost over, and winter comes early in these regions. Despite these facts, Caesar hastened to set out for Britain, aware as he was that our enemies in almost all our wars with the Gauls had received reinforcements from that quarter. He considered, moreover, that even if the season left no time for a campaign, none the less it would be a great advantage to him simply to land on the island and observe the kind of people who lived there, and the localities, harbours, and approaches. Every one of these points was unknown to almost all the Gauls.

No one, except for traders, went there as a matter of course, and not even they knew anything beyond the coastline and the areas facing Gaul. Thus, when Caesar summoned traders from every region he was unable to ascertain either the size of the island, the nature and numbers of the peoples living there, their skill in warfare, their established customs, or which harbours were suitable for a fleet of fairly large ships.

He needed information on all these matters, and he judged it appropriate to send Gaius Volusenus ahead with a warship. He gave Volusenus instructions to make a thorough reconnoitre and return to him as soon as possible. Then Caesar set out with all his forces for the territory of the Morini, from where the crossing to Britain was shortest. He gave orders for ships from the surrounding areas, together with the fleet which he had had constructed the previous summer for the campaign against the Veneti, to gather there. Meanwhile his plan became known, and traders relayed it to the Britons. Then envoys approached him from several of the island's communities: they promised to surrender hostages and to obey the rule of the Roman people. Caesar heard them, and made generous pledges, encouraging them to remain loyal to their avowed intentions. Volusenus had spied out the whole area as best he could. Then he returned to Caesar on the fifth day and reported what he had observed.

About eighty transport vessels were mustered and collected, a number Caesar considered sufficient to ferry two legions across. Besides this, he divided up the warships in his possession between his quaestor, legates, and prefects. There were also eighteen transport vessels approaching, but a strong wind was holding them back about seven miles off and preventing them from sailing into the same harbour: he assigned these to the cavalry.

de Bello Gallico 4.23

These matters settled, he took advantage of a spell of good weather for sailing and weighed anchor around the third watch. He ordered the cavalry to embark and follow him. He reached Britain with the first ships at around the fourth hour; there he spied the enemy forces, fully armed and drawn up all along the cliffs. Such was the geography of this place, and so steep the cliffs which bounded the sea, that it was possible for missiles cast from the heights to find their target on the shore. He judged this place wholly unsuitable for disembarkation, so waited at anchor until the rest of the fleet arrived at the ninth hour. Meanwhile he summoned his legates and military tribunes, and set out what he had learned from Volusenus and what he wanted done. After dismissing them and taking advantage of a favourable wind and tide together, he gave the signal and weighed anchor. He sailed about six and a half miles further on and landed on a flat and open shore.

de Bello Gallico 4.24–6

The barbarians, however, had grasped the Romans' strategy and sent their cavalry on ahead, and their charioteers (it is their usual custom to use chariots in battle). They followed on with the rest of their forces and prevented our men from disembarking. This led to extreme difficulties, because the ships were too large to be beached except in deep water, while the soldiers, ignorant of the land, their hands full, weighed down by the size and weight of their weapons, at one and the same time had to jump down from the ships, find their feet in the surf, and fight the enemy. The Britons, on the other hand, were either on dry ground or in shallow water, their limbs unencumbered, the ground very familiar. They cast missiles boldly and spurred on their horses, which were well used to such work. This led to panic among our men, who were wholly unaccustomed to this style of fighting, and thus did not display the same eagerness and enthusiasm as they habitually did in infantry engagements.

When Caesar observed this he gave orders for the warships to be moved a short distance from the transport vessels halted on the enemy's exposed flank. From there the enemy could be repelled and driven off with slings, arrows, and missiles. This act was of great assistance to our men. The barbarians were thrown into a panic by the appearance of the ships, the movement of the oars, and the unfamiliar type of missiles used. They halted and then retreated a short distance. Meanwhile our soldiers were hesitating, chiefly because the sea was so deep; then the man who carried the Eagle of the Tenth legion appealed to the gods to see that his action turned out well for the legion, and said: 'Jump down, soldiers, unless you want to betray our Eagle to the enemy – I at least shall have done my duty to the Republic and to my commander.' He cried these words in a loud voice, then flung himself away from the ship and began to carry the Eagle towards the enemy. Then our men urged each other to prevent such a disgrace and all together jumped down from the ship. When the men who were on the closest nearby ships saw them do this, they followed them and drew close to the enemy.

Both sides fought fiercely. None the less, our men could not keep ranks or get a firm foothold, neither were they able to follow the standards; rather, different men from different ships grouped round whatever standard they ran up against, and they were in great confusion. The enemy, however, knew all the shallows, so when they caught sight from the shore of some of our men disembarking one by one, they spurred their horses on and attacked while our men were still at a disadvantage, their many surrounding our few. Some began throwing weapons against a whole group of our men on their exposed side. When Caesar noticed this he gave orders for the boats of the warships and likewise the spy vessels to be filled with soldiers. Wherever he saw men struggling, there he dispatched assistance. As soon as our men stood on dry ground, closely followed by all their comrades, they charged the enemy and routed them; but they could not pursue them very far, because the cavalry had failed to hold its course and reach the island. This was the one action in which Caesar's previous good fortune was found lacking.

de Bello Gallico 4.27–9

The enemy had been beaten in battle. As soon as they recovered from the rout they at once sent envoys to Caesar to discuss peace terms. They promised to provide hostages and to do whatever he told them. In seeking peace, they blamed the common crowd for what had taken place and begged him to pardon their lack of judgement. Caesar complained that although of their own accord they had sent envoys to the Gallic mainland to seek peace, they had then started a war with no reason; then he declared a pardon for their lack of judgement and demanded hostages. A number of these were surrendered at once, others were summoned from outlying areas and, they claimed, would be handed over in a few days' time. Meanwhile they ordered their men to return to their lands, and their leaders began to assemble from all directions and commit themselves and their states to Caesar.

These acts established the peace. Four days after the arrival in Britain the eighteen ships which had transported the cavalry set sail with a gentle breeze and left port. When they were drawing near to Britain and were spied from the camp, suddenly a storm arose which was so fierce that not one of the ships could hold her course. Some were carried back to the place from which they had set out. Others, in terrible danger, were swept further down the island's coast, in a westerly direction.

As it happened there was a full moon that night. On this day the Ocean tides are usually at their highest – a fact of which our men were unaware. So at one and the same time the tide had flooded the warships which Caesar had beached, and the storm began to inflict damage on the transport vessels, which were fast at anchor. Nor did our men get any chance to bring them assistance. Several of the ships were wrecked, the rest had lost their ropes, their anchors, and the rest of their rigging, and were unfit to sail. The result was panic throughout the army. For there were no other ships to transport them back, and they had no materials of use for naval repairs. Moreover, no corn had been provided for wintering in Britain.

de Bello Gallico 4.30–34

Once they learned of this the British leaders who had approached Caesar after the battle held talks among themselves. They realized that the Romans had neither cavalry nor ships nor corn, and understood, from the smallness of the camp, their weakness in manpower. Thus they considered it the perfect moment to engineer a renewal of hostilities, to cut our men off from corn and supplies and prolong the action into the winter. They were confident of overcoming our men or cutting off their escape, and so ensuring that no one would ever again cross to Britain to wage war. So they plotted together once more, and began to leave camp, a few at a time, and to call their men back in secret from the fields.

Even though Caesar had not yet learned of their plans, none the less he suspected it would happen. So he began to prepare safeguards for every eventuality. Every day he gathered corn from the fields into the camp, and he used timber and bronze from the ships which had been most badly damaged to repair the rest. He gave orders for equipment to be ferried over from mainland Gaul for this purpose. The soldiers carried out these tasks with great enthusiasm, and so by the loss of twelve ships Caesar was able to render the rest sufficiently seaworthy.

While this was going on one legion had been sent out in a body as usual to find corn. As yet no hint of hostilities had occurred, since some of the Britons were still in the fields, while others were even making frequent visits to the Roman camp. Then the men on guard at the gates of the camp reported to Caesar that a dust-cloud, greater than usual, was visible in the place

to which the Seventh had marched. Caesar guessed the truth, that the barbarians had started upon some new stratagem. He gave orders for the cohorts which were then on guard to set out with him to the place: the rest were to arm themselves and follow him without delay. When they had made their way some distance from the camp he caught sight of his men being hard pressed by the enemy and struggling to hold their position. Missiles were being thrown at them from every quarter. Because all the corn had been cut from the remaining areas, and this place alone was left, the enemy had suspected that our men would come there and had hidden by night in the woods. Then, when our men were scattered and, busy cutting corn, had laid down their weapons, they suddenly attacked, killed a few, cast the remainder into disorder, and surrounded them at once with cavalry and chariots.

Because this type of fighting was so unusual our men were thrown into confusion by such tactics, but in the nick of time Caesar brought them assistance. For the enemy halted at his coming, while our men recovered from their panic. After this he considered that it was an inopportune moment for going on the offensive and engaging in battle, so he stayed where he was, and after a short while led the legions back to camp. During these events all our men were busy, and the rest of the Britons who were in the fields dispersed.

Continual storms followed for a number of days, which kept our men in camp and prevented the enemy from fighting. In the meantime the barbarians sent out messengers in all directions who proclaimed to their own people that our troops were few in number, and declared how great was the opportunity of winning booty and of liberating themselves for ever if they drove the Romans from their camp. In this way a high force of infantry and cavalry was quickly mustered and approached our camp.

de Bello Gallico 4.35–8

Caesar foresaw that the same thing would happen as on previous days, namely, that if they were repulsed the enemy would use speed to escape the danger. Nevertheless, he stationed his legions in battle formation in front of the camp. Battle was joined. The enemy was unable to withstand the attack of our soldiers for very long, and fled. Our men pursued for as far as their vigour and strength allowed, killed a number of them, then set fire to all the buildings far and wide and returned to camp.

On the same day the enemy sent envoys to Caesar to sue for peace. Caesar doubled the number of hostages which he had previously demanded from them and ordered that they be taken to the Gallic mainland, because the autumnal equinox was at hand and he considered that as his ships were damaged the voyage should not be exposed to winter storms. He took advantage of a period of good weather and set sail a little after midnight. All the ships reached the mainland safely. Following receipt of a dispatch from Caesar, a thanksgiving of twenty days was decreed by the Senate for these achievements.

2 The second invasion of Britain

de Bello Gallico 5.8–9

After these events Labienus was left on the mainland with three legions and 2,000 cavalry to watch over the harbours, see to the corn supply, and find out what was happening in Gaul. Caesar set out with five legions and the same number of cavalry as he had left on the mainland. He weighed anchor at sunset. A gentle south-westerly breeze carried him out, but around midnight it dropped and he could no longer maintain his course. He was then carried too far by the flood-tide, and at dawn saw Britain being left behind to port. Then he followed the ebb-tide back and rowed hard to reach that part of the island where he had found the best landing-places the previous summer. The whole fleet reached Britain at around midday, but there was no enemy visible in the area. Later, however, Caesar learned from prisoners that although a large host of them had arrived, they had panicked at the size of the fleet, which was seen to number more than 800 at once. So they had left the shore and hidden themselves away on higher ground.

The army landed and a suitable site for the camp was found. When Caesar learned from prisoners where the enemy forces were stationed he left ten cohorts and 300 cavalry on the shore to guard the fleet, and during the third watch set out against the enemy. He was the less concerned for the fleet because he was leaving it anchored along a sandy, low-lying coast. He put Quintus Atrius in charge of this garrison. During the night he advanced about twelve miles before catching sight of the enemy forces. They brought their cavalry and chariots forward from higher ground to a river and began to block the way of our men and to engage in fighting. They were forced back by our cavalry and hid in the forest, where they occupied a place which was strong in both natural and man-made defences. It was apparent that they had previously made this ready to serve in their domestic warfare, for every one of the entrances was blocked off by the felling of a large number of trees. They came out from the forest to fight in small detachments, and prevented our men from coming within the fortifications. But the men of the Seventh legion formed up into a 'tortoise', piled up a ramp against the fortifications, seized control of the stronghold, and drove the enemy from the forest. They themselves suffered few casualties. Caesar, however, forbade them to pursue the fugitives very far, both because he was not familiar with the terrain and because the day was already far spent, and he wanted there to be enough time left for fortifying the camp.

de Bello Gallico 5.10–11

The following morning he sent the soldiers and cavalry out in three divisions on a foray to pursue fugitives. After they had marched a considerable distance they caught sight of the enemy rearguard. Just then riders came to Caesar from Quintus Atrius and reported that a terrible storm had blown up the night before, and almost all the ships were damaged and cast up on the shore – for the anchors and ropes had failed, and so the sailors and helmsmen could not withstand the force of the storm. As a result, the ships had been dashed one against the other, and serious damage had resulted.

On learning this, Caesar ordered the legions and cavalry to be recalled and to maintain their resistance on the march. He himself returned to the ships. Then he saw everything for himself, almost exactly as he had heard it described by the messengers and dispatch. Yet although about forty ships were lost, it was apparent that with considerable labour the rest could be rebuilt. So he selected workmen from the legions and ordered more to be summoned from mainland Gaul. Then, despite the considerable difficulty and effort involved, Caesar decided the most convenient solution was to beach all the ships and join them with the camp by a single line of fortification. The work lasted for ten days: the soldiers had no break from their efforts even at night. Once the ships were beached and the camp strongly fortified, he left the same forces as before to guard the fleet and returned to the place he had left earlier.

de Bello Gallico 5.11, 15, 17

By the time of his arrival even larger British forces had mustered there. By common agreement they had entrusted the supreme command of their campaign to Cassivellaunus, whose lands were separated from the coastal states by a river called the Thames, which is about eighty miles from the sea. Between Cassivellaunus and the other states there had previously been continual warfare, but our arrival frightened the Britons into putting him in charge of the entire war effort.

The enemy cavalry and charioteers clashed fiercely in combat with our cavalry on the march, though the outcome showed that our men were superior in every respect and drove them into the woods and hills. Despite killing a number of the enemy, they pursued too eagerly and lost a number of their own side. After a short time, when our men were off guard and busy fortifying the camp, the Britons suddenly rushed out of the woods and attacked the guards stationed in front of the camp. A fierce fight ensued. Caesar sent two cohorts to their assistance – the primary cohorts of their respective legions – and they positioned themselves with only a very small gap to separate them. Because our men were frightened by the unfamiliar tactics, the enemy boldly broke through their midst and retreated without casualties. On that day the military tribune Quintus Laberius was killed. The Britons were driven back after more cohorts were sent in support.

The following day the enemy took up a position on high ground far from camp. They began to appear in small detachments and attack our cavalry, though less eagerly than the day before. At midday, though, when Caesar had sent three legions and all the cavalry with his legate Gaius Trebonius to forage for food, the enemy suddenly swept down upon the foragers from all directions with such force that they did not stop before coming up with the standards and the legions. Our legionaries attacked fiercely and drove them back; they did not halt the pursuit until the cavalry saw the legions behind them and had the confidence in their support to drive the enemy headlong. They cut down a large number, and allowed them no opportunity to rally or make a stand or jump down from their chariots. Directly after this battle the enemy reinforcements which had mustered all dispersed. Thereafter the Britons were never at full strength when they engaged with our forces.

de Bello Gallico 5.18–21

Caesar learned of their plans and led his army to the River Thames in the territory of Cassivellaunus. This river can only be crossed at a single spot, on foot, and then with difficulty. When he arrived, he observed the large enemy forces drawn up on the opposite bank, the surface of which was protected by a covering of sharpened stakes. Fixed beneath the water, similar stakes were concealed by the river. On learning these facts from prisoners and deserters, Caesar sent the cavalry on ahead and ordered the legions to follow up at once. The soldiers moved with such speed and vigour that – although they had only their heads above water – the enemy could not withstand the assault of the legions and cavalry, abandoned the river-bank, and took to their heels.

As we explained above, Cassivellaunus had given up all hope of a confrontation and dismissed the greater part of his forces, so that about 4,000 charioteers remained. He kept watch on our marches, withdrawing a short distance from the road and keeping himself hidden in difficult wooded terrain. Wherever he knew we would be marching, he forced men and livestock to leave the fields for the forest. Whenever our cavalry rushed into the fields, ranging too freely in search of plunder and devastation, he sent his charioteers by every path and track out of the woods: the clash between them brought our cavalry into great danger. Thus fear prevented them from ranging more widely. All that remained for Caesar was to forbid anyone straying too far from the column of legions, and to inflict as much harm upon the enemy – by ravaging the fields and starting fires – as the legionary soldiers could manage despite the exertion of the march.

Meanwhile the Trinobantes (one of the most powerful states in those parts) sent envoys to Caesar and promised to surrender to him and to obey his commands. Caesar demanded forty hostages from them, and corn for his army. They quickly carried out his commands, and sent the required number of hostages and the corn. Thus the Trinobantes were made secure, and protected from any harm at the soldiers' hands. Then the Cenimagni, Segontiaci, Ancalites, Bibroci, and Cassi sent embassies and put themselves under Caesar's protection. He learned from them that Cassivellaunus' strong-hold, which was protected by woods and marshes, was not far from his present location: he had gathered quite a large number of men and cattle there. Caesar made his way there with the legions, and found it a place with admirable natural and man-made defences. None the less, he exerted himself to attack it on two sides. The enemy lingered a short while, but did not withstand the assault of our soldiers, and burst out from another part of the stronghold. Large numbers of cattle were found there, and many of the enemy were caught as they fled and put to death.

de Bello Gallico 5.22

While all this was taking place in that area Cassivellaunus sent messengers to Kent (which, as we explained above, is by the sea). This was a region ruled over by four kings. He ordered them to muster all their forces, strike at the Roman fleet's camp without warning, and launch an assault. When they reached the camp, however, our men made a sortie. They killed a large number of the enemy and returned without casualties. News of this battle reached Cassivellaunus. He had suffered many defeats and his lands were ruined: he was particularly disturbed by the defection of allied states, so finally he sent envoys to Caesar to surrender. Caesar had decided to winter on the mainland for fear of sudden Gallic uprisings. He realized that not much of the summer remained, so he demanded hostages and settled the annual tribute which Britain must pay to the Roman people.

Revolt in Gaul 1: The ambush of Sabinus and Cotta

de Bello Gallico 5.26–7

About a fortnight after the arrival in winter quarters revolt and defection suddenly sprang up at the instigation of Ambiorix and Catuvolcus. Although they had presented themselves to Sabinus and Cotta on the borders of their kingdom, and had transported corn to the winter camp, messengers from Indutiomarus of the Treveri spurred them on to rouse their own people. They suddenly attacked the men who were sent to fetch wood and then pressed on in large numbers to the camp to assault it. Our men quickly seized their weapons and climbed the rampart, while the cavalry were dispatched from one direction and emerged the victors after a cavalry battle. The enemy abandoned hope and withdrew their men from the assault. Then in accordance with their custom they shouted for someone from our side to proceed to a parley: they wanted to say something, they claimed, which was to the advantage of all, and by means of which they hoped that these quarrels could be abated.

Gaius Arpineius was sent to parley with them. With him went Quintus Junius. In their presence Ambiorix spoke to the following effect: for all Caesar's marks of favour towards himself he admitted that he was very much obliged; for it was through Caesar's offices that he had been freed from the habitual payment of tribute to his neighbours, the Aduatuci. Also, Caesar had returned his son and his nephew. His action, he went on, in assaulting the camp was not undertaken of his own free will and decision, but under compulsion from the state, because it was unable to withstand a sudden Gallic conspiracy. The whole of Gaul, he went on, was in agreement. This was the day appointed for attacking all Caesar's winter camps, so that no one legion could come to the aid of another. Ambiorix warned Sabinus, he pleaded with him, to look to his own safety and that of his soldiers. A great host of Germans had been hired, and had crossed the Rhine – in two days it would be upon them. It was for Sabinus and Cotta to decide, said Ambiorix, whether they wished to take the men out of winter quarters before the neighbouring peoples were aware, and lead them either to Quintus Cicero or to Labienus, one of whom was about fifty miles away, the other a little more. Finally Ambiorix made this promise, and confirmed it with an oath – he would give them a safe passage through his land.

de Bello Gallico 5.28–30

Arpineius and Junius reported what they had heard to the legates, who were much disturbed by this sudden turn of events. Even if these were the words of an enemy, they still thought they should not be ignored. So they brought the matter before a council, where fierce disagreement arose between them. A number of the military tribunes and leading centurions thought that nothing should be done on the spur of the moment, and that they should not leave their winter quarters without orders from Caesar. They argued that the German forces, however large, could be held off if their winter camp were fortified. They were not short of corn supplies – in the meantime help would come both from the winter camps nearby and from Caesar.

Sabinus replied by protesting loudly that by the time the enemy hordes – their numbers swelled by German allies – had arrived, or some disaster had occurred in the winter camps nearby, it would be too late to do anything. Either way, his own view was safe – if nothing very untoward occurred, they would reach the nearest legion without risk; if, on the other hand, the whole of Gaul sided with the Germans, their only safety was in flight.

Following this argument for both views, Cotta and the centurions vigorously opposed Sabinus, but he raised his voice so that a large number of the soldiers could hear him, and said: 'Have it your own way if you must – I am not the man to fear the threat of death most of all among you. These soldiers will understand: if anything untoward happens, they will demand that you justify yourselves. After all, if only you would let them, the day after tomorrow they would join forces with the nearest camp and endure the hazard of war together with all the rest – instead of being isolated and exiled, to perish from hunger or the sword far from reinforcements.'

de Bello Gallico 5.31

They got up from the council, and their friends seized them both by the hand, pleading with them not to let their own stubborn disagreement jeopardize the outcome. Disagreement over this matter continued until midnight. Finally Cotta was moved to yield. Sabinus' view prevailed. It was announced that they would set out at dawn. At dawn they set out from the camp, convinced that the advice they had received came not from an enemy but from a true friend, Ambiorix. The column was a very long one, and its baggage extremely heavy.

de Bello Gallico 5.32–7

After the enemy realized, because of all the bustle and watchfulness, that the Romans were on their way, they set up ambushes at two locations in the woods and then began to await the Romans' arrival in a convenient hidden spot about two miles off. When the greater part of the column had descended into a deep ravine they suddenly appeared at both ends of it and began to attack the rearguard and stop the vanguard from climbing up, engaging with our men in a very unequal position.

Because he had anticipated nothing of the kind, it was only then that Sabinus finally showed some anxiety, and ran about arranging his cohorts. Even this he did fearfully, and as if all presence of mind were seen to fail him. This generally tends to happen to men who are obliged to make decisions in the midst of action. Cotta, on the other hand, had considered the possibility that this might happen during their march, and for that reason had not supported the proposal to leave camp. He began to do everything he could to secure the safety of all, and to perform the duties both of a commander (by calling on the men by name and encouraging them) and of an ordinary soldier (by taking part in the fighting). Because the column was so long, it was rather difficult for the commanders to keep a watch on everything and to anticipate what was needed at each point – so they gave orders to pass the word on to abandon the baggage and form a circle.

The barbarians, on the other hand, did not lack a strategy for reacting to this move. Their leaders gave orders to pass the word all down the line – no one was to leave his post: all the booty was theirs, and whatever the Romans left was set apart for them. In this way they believed everything would be staked on victory. Though abandoned by their commander and by fortune, our men still knew that in courage lay their only hope of safety. Whenever a cohort made a sally a large number of the enemy facing it fell. Once Ambiorix had noticed this he gave orders to pass the word that his men must throw their weapons from a distance, rather than approaching too close. He also told them to give ground wherever the Romans attacked. Encumbered as they were, our men still put up a resistance, receiving many wounds; the day was more than half over, and they had fought from dawn until the eighth hour without doing anything to disgrace themselves. Then Quintus Lucanius went to the assistance of his son, who was surrounded, and died fighting courageously. The legate Lucius Cotta, whilst urging on all the cohorts and ranks, was wounded by a stone from a sling which hit him full in the face.

All this threw Sabinus into a panic. He saw Ambiorix from a distance urging on his men, and sent a messenger to ask him to spare himself and the Roman soldiers. Ambiorix responded to this appeal by saying that Sabinus was free to parley if he wished. Sabinus reported all this to the wounded Cotta, to get his agreement to the two of them leaving the battle and holding a parley with Ambiorix. He hoped his request to Ambiorix for safety for themselves and their men would be successful. Cotta said that he would not approach an armed enemy, and persisted in this opposition.

Then Sabinus ordered the military tribunes presently at his side to follow him. When he approached Ambiorix he was told to throw down his weapons: he did as he was told, and ordered his men to do the same. In the meantime, while they negotiated terms, Sabinus was gradually surrounded and killed. Then indeed they proclaimed the victory after their own fashion by raising a howl, made an attack on our ranks, and scattered them. There Lucius Cotta fell fighting, together with most of our soldiers. The rest retreated to the camp they had left behind. They barely managed to keep up the fight until nightfall – and when it was dark they abandoned hope of saving themselves and every single one of them committed suicide. A few men who had slipped away from the battle made their way by a haphazard route through the forest to the legate Titus Labienus and his winter quarters. They informed him of all that had occurred.

Revolt in Gaul 2: The siege of Cicero's camp

de Bello Gallico 5.38–9

Ambiorix was ecstatic at this victory. Straight away he set out with his cavalry for the land of the Aduatuci, which bordered his own kingdom. He marched for a day and a night without resting, and ordered the infantry to follow on. Once he had described what happened the Aduatuci were thoroughly roused. Next day he approached the Nervii and urged them not to let slip a chance to liberate themselves forever and inflict vengeance on the Romans for the wrongs they had suffered at their hands. He explained that two legates had been killed and a large part of the army had perished: it would be no trouble at all to attack the legion wintering under Quintus Cicero and annihilate it. His words easily convinced the Nervii.

Accordingly messengers were dispatched at once to the Ceutrones, Grudii, Levaci, Pleumoxii, and Geidumni, who were all under Nervian rule. They mustered the greatest forces they could and rushed without warning to the winter camp of Quintus Cicero, who had not yet received news of Sabinus' death. Inevitably it befell Quintus Cicero, as it also had Sabinus, that some of his soldiers who had gone into the woods in search of timber for the defences were cut off by the sudden arrival of enemy cavalry. They were surrounded, and a vast host of Eburones, Nervii, Aduatuci, and their allies and dependants began to attack the legion. Our men swiftly ran to arms and climbed up the rampart. They barely got through the day, for the enemy's hopes were all pinned on a swift result, and they were sure that once this victory was won they would be conquerors for ever.

de Bello Gallico 5.40–43

Quintus Cicero at once sent a dispatch to Caesar, and promised the bearers great reward if they got it through. But all the roads were blockaded, and the messengers were intercepted. That night, with astonishing speed, our men constructed towers – a full 120 of them – out of the timber which they had gathered for the defences. Any defects apparent in the defences were corrected. Next day the enemy attacked the camp in much greater numbers, and filled in the ditch. Our men resisted in the same way as the day before. Day after day the same thing happened. At no time of night was there any break from work: neither the sick nor the wounded were given a chance to rest. Whatever was needed for the next day's fighting was prepared by night. Cicero himself was in poor health, but did not even allow himself rest at night; eventually he was compelled to spare his exertions by the pressure and insistence of his soldiers.

Now the commanders and leaders of the Nervii declared that they wanted to parley with Cicero. Once the opportunity was granted they enumerated the same arguments as Ambiorix had used with Sabinus, namely, that the whole of Gaul was up in arms, the Germans had crossed the Rhine, and the winter camps of Caesar and the others were under attack. They also reminded him of Sabinus' death. They said they would permit the Romans to depart from their camp unharmed and go wherever they wanted without fear. Quintus Cicero made only one reply to this speech – it was not the Roman people's custom, he said, to accept terms from an armed enemy. If they were willing to lay down their weapons he would offer them assistance in sending envoys to Caesar.

The Nervii had hoped to entrap him, but were thus rebuffed. They now encircled the camp with a nine-foot rampart and a ditch fifteen feet wide. During the days which remained they began to make ready and construct towers (in proportion to the height of the rampart), siege-hooks, and shelters. On the seventh day of the siege a stormy wind blew up. The Nervii started using slings to fire burning darts on to the soldiers' cabins, which were thatched in Gallic fashion. They quickly caught fire, and because the wind was so strong the blaze spread into every part of the camp. The enemy gave a great shout as if they were certain of a victory already won, and began to mobilize the towers and shelters, and to use ladders to scale the rampart. Everywhere our soldiers were scorched by the flames and harassed by a cascade of missiles, and they realized that all their baggage and their property was being reduced to ashes. Nevertheless, such was the bravery of our soldiers, and their firm resolution, that not only did none of them abandon the rampart to make his escape but not one of them even so much as looked back. Instead they all fought as fiercely and as bravely as they could. This day was by far the hardest for our men, but it still resulted in a very large number of the enemy being wounded or killed, for they had crowded together under the actual rampart, and so the rearward ranks gave those in front no opportunity to withdraw. Indeed, when there was a short lull in the fire, in one place a tower was brought up to touch the rampart. Then the centurions of the third cohort retreated from where they were stationed and moved back all their men. They began to beckon and call to the enemy to enter if they so wished. Not one of them did dare to make the advance. In fact, stones thrown from all directions brought them tumbling down, and the tower was set on fire.

de Bello Gallico 5.44

In this legion there were two centurions, both men of great courage. Their names were Titus Pullo and Lucius Vorenus. There was always a dispute going on between them as to which had precedence over the other, and every year they clashed in fierce rivalry over the most important posts. While the fighting at the defences was at its height Pullo shouted: 'Why are you hesitating, Vorenus? What chance are you waiting for of winning praise for your bravery? This day will decide the contest between us.' With these words he made his way outside the defences and launched an attack where the enemy ranks were densest. Nor indeed did Vorenus remain within the rampart, but followed his rival for fear of what men would think of him. Then Pullo cast his spear against the enemy at close range, and transfixed a Gaul who had run forward from the ranks. He was knocked senseless, so they covered him with their shields and all together threw their weapons at Pullo, giving him no opportunity to withdraw. Pullo's shield was pierced, and a dart was stuck in his swordbelt – this knocked his sheath and hindered his attempt to draw his sword. While he was in difficulties the enemy surrounded him. To the rescue came Vorenus, his rival, who helped him out of trouble. Straight away the Gauls turned their attention from Pullo to Vorenus, thinking the former had been killed by the dart. With his sword Vorenus fought at close quarters. He killed one man, and drove the rest off a short way. But he pressed forward too eagerly, tripped, and fell into a hollow. Now he was surrounded, and Pullo came to his aid. They killed several Gauls and both returned safely within the defences to great acclaim. Thus fortune played with them both in their rivalry and struggle, so that despite their enmity each helped and saved the other, and it was impossible to decide which should be considered the braver of the two.

de Bello Gallico 5.45–6

The siege became more grim and relentless day by day. As the situation worsened more and more dispatches and messengers were sent off to Caesar: some of the messengers were caught and tortured in the sight of our men, and then put to death. Within the camp was a well-born Nervian called Vertico, who had fled to Quintus Cicero for refuge at the start of the siege, and had proved his loyalty to him. He used the hope of freedom and large rewards to persuade one of his slaves to carry a dispatch to Caesar. The slave got the message out attached to a spear, and by mingling freely as a Gaul among Gauls without arousing suspicion he made his way to Caesar. Through him the threat to Quintus Cicero and his legion was discovered.

Caesar received the dispatch at about the eleventh hour of the day, and at once sent a messenger to the territory of the Bellovaci, to Marcus Crassus whose winter camp was about twenty-five miles away. He ordered Crassus' legion to set out at midnight and come quickly to him. As soon as the messenger arrived Crassus set out. Caesar sent a second messenger to Gaius Fabius, telling him to take his legion to the territory of the Atrebates, through which he knew that he too must march. He wrote to Labienus and told him to bring his legion into Nervian territory if it was possible without endangering the common good. He thought it best not to wait for the rest of the army, which was some distance away. He mustered about 400 cavalry from the winter camps nearby.

de Bello Gallico 5.47–8

At about the third hour outriders came to tell him that Crassus was arriving. On that day he advanced twenty miles. He put Crassus in charge of Samarobriva and allocated him a legion, because this was where he was leaving behind the army's baggage, the nations' hostages, state documents, and all the corn which he had transported there to provide food throughout the winter. After a short delay Fabius and his legion (as ordered) met Caesar on the march. Labienus had received news of the death of Sabinus and the slaughter of his cohorts. Now that all the forces of the Treviri had come upon him, he was afraid that if he set out from his camp it would look as if he was fleeing, and he would be unable to withstand an enemy attack. So he wrote to Caesar, explaining how risky it would be to lead his legion out of winter camp. He described how all the infantry and cavalry forces of the Treviri had taken up position three miles from his own camp.

Caesar approved his judgement. Despite the fact that his hope of having three legions was dashed, and he was now reduced to two, he none the less regarded speed as the only means of securing the safety of all. By forced marches he reached Nervian territory. There he learned from prisoners what was happening with Quintus Cicero, and how dangerous the situation was. Then he persuaded one of the Gallic cavalry, by means of a large bribe, to convey a letter to Quintus Cicero. The dispatch he sent was written in Greek so that if it was intercepted the enemy could not discover our plans. If this Gaul was unable to reach him, Caesar told him to hurl a throwing spear inside the camp defences, with the letter tied to its strap. In it he wrote that he was on his way with the legions and would soon be there; and he urged Quintus Cicero to keep up his former courage. The Gaul did fear a threat, and so cast his spear as ordered. By chance it stuck in one of our towers. Unnoticed by our men for two days, on the third it was finally spotted by one of the soldiers, removed, and taken to Quintus Cicero. He scanned it through, then read it aloud to an assembly of the troops: this gave rise to great delight among them all. Then, far off, the smoke of burnings was spied, and this put an end to doubt that the legions were at hand.

de Bello Gallico 5.49

When the Gauls learned from scouts what was happening they abandoned the siege, and set out against Caesar with all their forces. These totalled about 60,000 men under arms. When the opportunity offered, Quintus Cicero asked the same Vertico as we mentioned above for a Gaul to convey a dispatch to Caesar. He warned this man to make his way carefully and with caution. In this letter he described in full how the enemy had departed from him, and had turned their entire force against Caesar. This dispatch reached Caesar at about midnight: he told his men what the situation was, and encouraged them for the fight. At dawn the following day he struck camp and marched for about four miles before the enemy army was spotted across a valley with a stream in it. It would be very risky to engage on unfavourable ground with so small a force; besides, he knew that Quintus Cicero was free of the pressure of the siege, so he could accept with equanimity the need to slacken the speed of his march. He halted and fortified a camp in the most advantageous position possible. The camp was already small in itself (numbering scarcely 7,000 men); even so, by making the roadways as narrow as possible he constricted it further, intending to make the enemy treat it with utter derision.

de Bello Gallico 5.50–52

That day there were minor cavalry engagements by the waterside, but both sides held their positions. The Gauls were awaiting larger forces which had not yet arrived, but Caesar hoped to lure the enemy on to his own ground by pretending to be afraid, and so to engage on his side of the valley in front of the camp. At dawn the enemy cavalry approached the camp and engaged in battle with our cavalry. Caesar ordered them to give ground on purpose, and retreat to the camp. At the same time he gave orders for the camp to be fortified with a higher rampart on all sides, and the gate to be barricaded – and for these tasks to be carried out with as much rushing about and pretence of panic as possible.

All these factors lured the enemy into bringing their forces over and forming up for battle on disadvantageous ground. Our men had even been withdrawn from the rampart, so they came closer and threw missiles inside the fortifications from all sides. Then they sent heralds all round the camp and told them to announce that any Gaul or Roman who wanted to come over to them before the third hour was free to do so unharmed. So deeply did they despise our men that some began to tear down the rampart with their hands, others to fill in the ditches. Then Caesar made a sortie from all the gates, let loose the cavalry, and routed the enemy so swiftly that not a single enemy Gaul halted to resist. He killed a large number of them and stripped them all of their arms.

He was reluctant to pursue them very far, for there were woods and marshes in the way. That same day, all his forces intact, he arrived at Quintus Cicero's camp. He called a parade of the legion, and learned that not so much as one soldier in ten was unwounded. All this led him to conclude how great had been their danger, and their courage in dealing with what had happened. He praised both Quintus Cicero and his legion as they deserved; then, one by one, he addressed the centurions and military tribunes, of whose outstanding bravery he had heard from Quintus Cicero. From the prisoners he learned for certain of the disaster which had befallen Sabinus and Cotta. The next day he held an assembly and related what had happened, offering comfort and reassurance to the soldiers. He told them to bear this loss, incurred through the rash fault of his legate, with greater equanimity because amends had been made for the set-back both by the assistance of the immortal gods and by their own courage. The enemy was left with no lasting cause for celebration, nor would their own grief be lasting.

Catullus

1

Whom do I give a neat new booklet
Polished up lately with dry pumice?
You, Cornelius; for you always
Thought my trivia important,
Even when you dared (the one Italian)
Unfold the whole past in three papyri –
Learned, by Jupiter, and laborious!
So take this mere booklet for what it's worth,
Which may my Virgin Patroness
Keep fresh for more than one generation.

1 Catullus and his friends

50

At leisure, Licinius, yesterday
We'd much fun with my writing-tablets
As we'd agreed to be frivolous.
Each of us writing light verses
Played now with this metre, now that,
Capping each other's jokes and toasts.
Yes, and I left there fired by
Your charm, Licinius, and wit,
So food gave poor me no pleasure
Nor could I rest my eyes in sleep
But wildly excited turned and tossed
Over the bed, longing for daylight
That I might be with you and talk.
But after my tired aching limbs
Were lying on the couch half dead,
I made this poem for you, the charmer,
So you could spot my trouble from it.
Now don't be rash, please – don't reject
Our prayers, we implore you, precious,
Lest Nemesis make you pay for it.
She's a drastic Goddess. Don't provoke her.

53

I laughed at someone in court lately
Who, when my Calvus gave a splendid
Account of all Vatinius' crimes,
With hands raised in surprise announced
'Great Gods, the squirt's articulate!'

49

Most eloquent of Romulus's grandsons
That are and have been, Marcus Tullius,
And ever will be in other years,

Catullus, the worst poet of all,
Sends you herewith his greatest thanks,
As truly the worst poet of all
As you're best advocate of all.

93

I am none too keen to wish to please you, Caesar,
    Nor to know if you're a white man or a black.

14

Did I not love you more than my eyes,
Calvus you joker, then for that gift
I'd hate you with Vatinian hatred.
What have I done to you or said
That you should pip me with all these poets?
May Gods bring curses on the client
Who sent you such profanities.
And if, as I suspect, this choice new
Gift to you is from schoolmaster Sulla,
Then I'm not sorry but delighted
That your hard work has not been wasted.
Great Gods, a damned awful little book
For you to send to your Catullus
To kill him outright on that day
Of all days best – the Saturnalia.
No, you won't get away with it,
Clever dick. When it's dawn I'll run
To the bookstalls, pick up all the poison –
Suffenus, Caesius and Aquinus –
And pay you back with pains like them.
Meanwhile goodbye, be off with you,
Back where you brought your faulty feet from,
Curse of our time, appalling poets!

9

Veranius, of all my friends
The foremost by three hundred miles,
Have you come home to your household Gods
And like-minded brothers and old mother?
You have? O happy news for me!
I'll find you safe, hear you describing
Iberian places, exploits, tribes
In your own fashion. Embracing you
I'll kiss your merry face and eyes.
O of all the happier people
Who's happier or more glad than I?

13

You'll dine well, my Fabullus, at mine
One day soon if the Gods are kind to you,
If you will bring with you a dinner

Good and large plus a pretty girl
And wine and salt and all the laughs.
If, I repeat, you bring these with you,
Our charmer, you'll dine well; for your
Catullus' purse is full of cobwebs.
But in return you'll get love neat
Or something still more choice and fragrant;
For I'll provide the perfume given
My girl by Venuses and Cupids
And when you smell it you'll ask the Gods,
Fabullus, to make you one large nose.

2 Catullus in love

51

That man is seen by me as a God's equal
Or (if it may be said) the Gods' superior,
Who sitting opposite again and again
Watches and hears *you*

Sweetly laughing – which dispossesses poor me
Of all my senses, for no sooner, Lesbia,
Do I look at you than there's no power left me
(Of speech in my mouth,)

But my tongue's paralysed, invisible flame
Courses down through my limbs, with din of their
    own
My ears are ringing and twin darkness covers
The light of my eyes.

2

Sparrow, my girl's darling,
Whom she plays with, whom she cuddles,
Whom she likes to tempt with finger-
Tip and teases to nip harder
When my own bright-eyed desire
Fancies some endearing fun
And a small solace for her pain,
I suppose, so heavy passion then rests:
Would I could play with you as she does
And lighten the spirit's gloomy cares!

3

Grieve, O Venuses and Loves
And all the lovelier people there are:
My girl's sparrow is dead,
Sparrow, my girl's darling,
Whom she loved more than her eyes.
For honey-sweet he was and knew his
Mistress well as a girl her mother.

Nor would he ever leave her lap
But hopping around, this way, that way,
Kept cheeping to his lady alone.
And now he's off on the dark journey
From which they say no one returns.
Shame on you, shameful dark of Orcus,
For gobbling up all the pretty things!
You've robbed me of so pretty a sparrow.
O what a shame! O wretched sparrow!
Your fault it is that now my girl's
Eyelids are swollen red with crying.

5

We should live, my Lesbia, and love
And value all the talk of stricter
Old men at a single penny.
Suns can set and rise again;
For us, once our brief light has set,
There's one unending night for sleeping.
Give me a thousand kisses, then a hundred,
Then another thousand, then a second hundred,
Then still another thousand, then a hundred;
Then, when we've made many thousands,
We'll muddle them so as not to know
Or lest some villain overlook us
Knowing the total of our kisses.

43

Greetings, girl with no mini nose
Nor pretty foot nor dark eyes
Nor long fingers nor dry mouth
Nor altogether felicitous tongue,
Friend of the bankrupt from Formiae.
And does the Province call you pretty?
Compare our Lesbia to you?
O what tasteless boorish times!

109

You give me hope this mutual love of ours, my life,
    Will be delightful and for ever.
Great Gods, enable her to promise truly,
    To say it honestly and from the heart,
That we may be allowed to keep lifelong
    This lasting pact of sacred friendship.

70

My woman says there's no one she would rather wed
    Than me, not even if asked by Jove himself.
Says – but what a woman says to an eager lover
    One should write on the wind and the running
                                                    water.

72

You said one day you only knew Catullus, Lesbia,
    And you'd refuse to embrace even Jove instead of
                                                    me.
I loved you then, not only as common men their
                                                    girlfriend
    But as a father loves his sons and sons-in-law.
I know you now. So though my passion's more
                                                    intense,
    Yet for me you're much cheaper and lighter-
                                                    weight.
'How can that be?' you ask. It's because such hurt
                                                    compels
    A lover to love more but to like less.

85

I hate and love. Perhaps you're asking why I do that?
    I don't know, but I feel it happening, and am
                                                    racked.

8

Wretched Catullus, you should stop fooling
And what you know you've lost admit losing.
The sun shone brilliantly for you, time was,
When you kept following where a girl led you,
Loved by us as we shall love no one.
There when those many amusing things happened
Which you wanted nor did the girl not want
The sun shone brilliantly for you, truly.
Now she's stopped wanting, you must stop,
    weakling.
Don't chase what runs away nor live wretched
But with a mind made up be firm, stand fast.
Goodbye, girl. Catullus now stands fast,
Won't ask or look for you who're not willing.
But you'll be sorry when you're not asked for.
Alas, what life awaits you now, devil?
Who'll find you pretty now? What type touch you?
Whom will you love and whose be called
    henceforth?
Whom will you kiss? and you will bite whose lips?
But you, Catullus, mind made up, stand fast.

76

If in recalling former kindnesses there's pleasure
    When a man reflects that he has been true
Nor broken solemn promise nor in any pact
    Abused the Gods' goodwill to fool his fellow men,
Then many joys remain in store for you, Catullus,
    Through a long lifetime from this ungrateful love.

For whatever kind things men can say or do
    To anyone, these you have said and done,
But credited to ingratitude they have all been wasted.
    So now why torture yourself any more?
Why not harden your heart and tear yourself away
    And stop being wretched against the Gods' will?
It's difficult to break with long love suddenly.
    It's difficult, but this you must somehow do.
This is your only chance. You must win through to
                    this.
    Possible or not, this you must achieve.
O Gods, if you can pity or have ever brought
    Help at last to any on the point of death,
Look on my wretchedness and if I have led a decent
                    life
    Take away from me this deadly disease,
Which like a paralysis creeping into my inmost being
    Has driven from my heart every happiness.
I do not ask now that she love me in return
    Or, what's impossible, that she be chaste.
I pray for my own health, to be rid of this foul
                 sickness.
    O Gods, grant me this for my true dealing.

77

Rufus, believed my friend in vain and all for nothing,
    (For nothing? No, to my great cost and sorrow)
Is this how you've crept up on me, burnt through my
                   guts
    And robbed poor me of all I value?
Yes, you've robbed me, alas, cruel poison of our life,
    Alas, the canker on our friendship.

Cicero: pro Caelio 49–50

If any unmarried woman has opened up her house to
everyone's lust and has openly set herself up in the life
of a whore, if she were to do this in the city, in her
garden, in all those crowds at Baiae, and finally if she
were to conduct herself not just by the way she walked
but by her get-up and her companions, not (just) by the
flashing of her eyes, not by the permissiveness of her
conversation, but also by her manner of embracing, her
way of kissing, her beach parties, her yachting parties,
her dinner parties – (conduct herself) in such a manner
that she appears not only a whore but also a shameless
whore: if some young man happens to be with this
woman, would he seem to you, Lucius Herennius, to be
an adulterer or a lover? I now forget the wrongs you did
me, Clodia, I lay aside the recollection of my distress; I
disregard the brutal actions you took against my friends
and family when I was abroad; let us suppose that what
I said was not said against you. But I want to know

from you yourself ... if there were any woman of such a
kind as I described a little before this, unlike you, a
whore by her set way of life, (and) a young man had
some dealings with her, whether this would seem
absolutely disgraceful and scandalous to you.

3 The sequel

11

Furius and Aurelius, Catullus' comrades,
Whether he'll push on to furthest India
Where the shore is pounded by far-resounding
Eoan rollers,

To Hyrcania or effeminate Arabia,
The Sacians or the arrow-bearing Parthians
Or those levels to which the seven-double
Nilus gives colour,

Or make his way across the towering Alps
To visit the memorials of great Caesar,
The Gallic Rhine, those horrible woad-painted
And world's end Britons –

All this, whatever the will of Heaven above
May bring, ready as you are to brave together,
Simply deliver to my girl a brief dis-
courteous message:

Farewell and long life with her adulterers,
Three hundred together, whom hugging she holds,
Loving none truly but again and again
Rupturing all's groins;

And let her not as before expect my love,
Which by her fault has fallen like a flower
On the meadow's margin after a passing
Ploughshare has touched it.

46

Now spring brings back unfrozen warmth,
Now the sky's equinoctial fury
Is hushed by Zephyr's welcome airs.
Take leave of Phrygian plains, Catullus,
And sweltering Nicaea's lush fields.
Let's fly to Asia's famous cities.
Excited thoughts now long to travel;
Glad feet now tap in expectation.
Farewell, sweet company of comrades,
Who leaving distant home together
Return by different routes apart.

101

Travelling through many nations and through many
                                seas
    I have come, brother, for these poor funeral rites,
That I might render you the last dues of the dead
    And vainly comfort your dumb ashes,
Because Fortune has robbed me of your self, alas,
    Poor brother, unfairly taken from me.
But now, meanwhile, accept these gifts which by old
                                 custom
    Of the ancestors are offered in sad duty
At funeral rites, gifts drenched in a brother's tears,
    And forever, brother, greetings and farewell.

31

Of almost islands, Sirmio, and islands
The jewel – of all that either Neptune bears
In clear lake-water or desolate ocean,
How pleased, how happy I am to see you again,
Hardly convinced that I have left Thynia
And the Bithynian plains and found you safe.
O what more blissful than to have no worries,
When mind lays down the load, and tired of foreign
Service we have come to our own Lar
And rest content upon the longed-for bed!
This on its own makes up for all the hardship.
Greetings, delightful Sirmio. Enjoy your
Master's joy, and you, the lake's Lydian waves,
Laugh with all the mirth you have at home.

4

The sailing-boat you see there, visitors,
Claims to have been the speediest of ships
And not to have been incapable of passing
Any swimming timber if need be
By flying with either little palms or canvas.
And he denies the threatening Adriatic
Coast can deny this, the Cycladic islands,
Famous Rhodes, Propontis shivering
In Thracian gales or the grim Pontic gulf
Where he, the future boat, was first of all
A long-haired wood; for on Cytorus' top
His hair would often speak in a loud whisper.
Pontic Amastris and box-clad Cytorus,
To you these things were best known and still are,
The boat claims. In his distant origin
He says it was your summit that he stood on,
Your sea in which he dipped his little palms,
And from there through so many stormy straits
Carried his master, whether from left or right

The breeze was calling, or a following
Jupiter fell upon both feet at once.
Nor were there any vows to the shore Gods
Made for him as he voyaged finally
From the open sea right up to this clear lake.
But that was in the past; now he grows old
In quiet retirement and devotes himself
To you, twin Castor, and you, Castor's twin.

10

Free in the Forum I was taken
By my Varus to meet his love,
A tartlet, as I thought at first,
By no means unwitty or unattractive.
Once arrived there we got talking
On various topics, including
Bithynia – how were things there now
And had it made me any brass?
I answered straight – there was nothing now
For praetors themselves or their staff,
Why anyone should come back flusher,
Especially when a shit's your praetor,
Who doesn't give a toss for staff.
'But surely' they said 'you collected
What's said to be the local product –
Bearers?' Whereat, to make the girl
Think me one of the luckier ones,
I said 'Things weren't so bad for me
Despite my drawing a bad province
That I could miss eight straight-backed men.'
In fact I'd no one, here or there,
To heave up on his head the broken
Leg of a second-hand camp-bed.
At this she said, like the bitch she was,
'Lend them to me, please, dear Catullus,
Just for a little. I need taking
To Sérapis.' 'Wait,' I replied
'What I said just now I had, I
Wasn't thinking. It's my messmate
Cinna – Gaius, you know – they're his.
But what's it matter whose they are?
I use them as if they were mine.
But you're damned tactless – a living nuisance
Who won't allow one to speak loosely.'

Virgil

1 Aeneas arrives at Carthage

Aeneid 1.12–22, 29–33

There was a town of old – men from Tyre colonized it
Over against Italy and Tiber mouth, but afar off,
Carthage, rich in resources, fiercely efficient in
    warfare.
This town, they say, was Juno's favourite dwelling,
    preferred
To all lands, even Samos: here were her arms, her
    chariot:
And even from the long-ago time she cherished the
    aim that this
Should be, if fate allowed, the metropolis of all
    nations.
Nevertheless, she had heard a future race was forming
Of Trojan blood, which one day would topple that
    Tyrian stronghold –
A people arrogant in war, born to be everywhere rulers
And root up her Libyan empire – so the Destiny-
    Spinners planned.
Furious at these things too, she tossed all over the sea
The Trojans, the few that the Greeks and relentless
    Achilles had left,
And rode them off from their goal, Latium. Many
    years
They were wandering round the seven seas, moved on
    by destiny.
So massive a task it was found the Roman race.

Aeneid 1.338–66

The kingdom you see is Carthage, the Tyrians, the
    town of Agenor;
But the country around is Libya, no folk to meet in
    war.
Dido, who left the city of Tyre to escape her brother,
Rules here – a long and labyrinthine tale of wrong
Is hers, but I will touch on its salient points in order.
Her husband was Sychaeus, a man of great estates
Among the Phoenicians and greatly loved by the ill-
    starred Dido
Whose father had given her in marriage to Sychaeus,
A virgin bride. Now the throne of Tyre was held by her
    brother,
Pygmalion, a monster who had no rival in wickedness.
Maniac evil stepped in. Pygmalion, blinded by love for
Gold, godlessly murdered the unsuspecting Sychaeus
In secret before the altar – no pang of compunction for
    her love;
And kept the deed dark for a long time, vilely
    inventive of fictions

To cheat with hollow hope her pining, loving heart.
But there came, one night as she slept, the phantom of
    her unburied
Husband, weirdly floating its clay-white face up to her,
Exposed the atrocious altar, the breast spitted with
    steel,
And took the cover off that crime hidden in the house.
Then the phantom urged her swiftly to fly the country,
And told her where she could find in the earth an old
    treasure, a secret
Hoard of gold and silver to help her on her way.
Dido, in great disquiet, organized her friends for
    escape.
They met together, all those who harshly hated the
    tyrant
Or keenly feared him: they seized some ships which
    chanced to be ready
And loaded them with the gold: so was that treasure
    sailed
Out of Pygmalion's grasp: a woman led the exploit.
They came to this spot, where today you can behold
    the mighty
Battlements and the rising citadel of New Carthage.

Aeneid 1.418–38

Meanwhile the two pressed on apace, where the track
    pointed.
And now they were climbing a hill whose massive
    bulk looms over
The city and commands a prospect of soaring towers.
Aeneas marvels at great buildings, where once were
    shanties,
Marvels at city gates and the din of the paved streets.
The Tyrians are busy at work there, some extending
    the walls,
Manhandling blocks of stone and building the citadel,
Others choosing a site for a house and trenching
    foundations:
Laws are being made, magistrates and a parliament
    elected:
Here they dig out a harbour basin; here they are laying
Foundations deep for a theatre, and hewing from stone
    immense
Columns to grace one day a tall proscenium.
So in the youth of summer throughout the flowering
    land
The bees pursue their labours under the sun: they lead
A young brood from the hive, or press the flowing
    honey
And fill the cells to bursting with a delicious nectar;
Relieve incoming bees of their burden, or closing ranks
Shoo the drones, that work-shy gang, away from the
    bee-folds.
The work goes on like wild-fire, the honey smells of

thyme.
Ah, fortunate you are, whose town is already building!
Aeneas said, and gazed up at the city's heights.

Aeneid 1.494–508

Now while Aeneas viewed with wonder all these
  scenes,
And stood at gaze, rooted in a deep trance of attention,
There came in royal state to the temple, a crowd of
  courtiers
Attending her, queen Dido, most beautiful to see.
As, by the banks of Eurotas or over the Cynthian
  slopes
Diana foots the dance, and a thousand Oreads
  following
Weave a constellation around that arrowy one,
Who in grace of movement excels all goddesses,
And happiness runs through the still heart of Latona –
So Dido was, even so she went her radiant way
Through the crowds, eager to forward the work and
  growth of her realm.
Now, at the holy doors, under the temple porch,
Hedged by the spears of her guard, she throned herself
  on high;
Gave laws and ordinances, appointed the various tasks
In equitable proportions or else by drawing lots.

2 The love of Dido and Aeneas

Aeneid 4.1–5

But now for some while the queen had been growing
  more grievously love-sick,
Feeding the wound with her life-blood, the fire biting
  within her.
Much did she muse on the hero's nobility, and much
On his family's fame. His look, his words had gone to
  her heart
And lodged there: she could get no peace from love's
  disquiet.

Aeneid 4.65–89

Ah, little the soothsayers know! What value have vows
  or shrines
For a woman wild with passion, the while love's flame
  eats into
Her gentle flesh and love's wound works silently in her
  breast?
So burns the ill-starred Dido, wandering at large
  through the town

In a rage of desire, like a doe pierced by an arrow – a
  doe which
Some hunting shepherd has hit with a long shot while
  unwary
She stepped through the Cretan woods, and all
  unknowing has left his
Winged weapon within her: the doe runs fleetly around
  the Dictaean
Woods and clearings, the deathly shaft stuck deep in
  her flank.
Now she conducts Aeneas on a tour of the city, and
  shows him
The vast resources of Carthage, the home there ready
  and waiting;
Begins to speak, then breaks off, leaving a sentence
  unfinished.
Now, as the day draws out, she wants to renew that
  first feast,
In fond distraction begs to hear once again the Trojan
Story, and hangs on his words as once again he tells it.
Then, when the company's broken up, when the moon
  is dimming
Her beams in turn and the dipping stars invite to sleep,
Alone she frets in the lonely house, lies down on her
  bed,
Then leaves it again: he's not there, not there, but she
  hears him and sees him.
Or charmed by his likeness to his father, she keeps
  Ascanius
Long in her lap to assuage the passion she must not
  utter.
Work on the half-built towers is closed down
  meanwhile; the men
Of Carthage have laid off drilling, or building the
  wharves and vital
Defences of their town; the unfinished works are idle –
Great frowning walls, head-in-air cranes, all at a
  standstill.

Aeneid 4.129–36, 138–72

So now, as Aurora was rising out of her ocean bed
And the day-beam lofted, there sallied forth the élite of
  Carthage:
With fine-meshed nets and snares and the broad
  hunting lances
Massylian riders galloped behind a keen-nosed pack.
The queen dallies: the foremost Carthaginians await
  her
By the palace door, where stands her horse,
  caparisoned
In purple and gold, high-spirited, champing the foam-
  flecked bit.
At last she comes, with many courtiers in attendance:

Her quiver is gold, her hair bound up with a golden
  clasp,
A brooch of gold fastens the waist of her brilliant
  dress.
Her Trojan friends were there too, and young Ascanius
In high glee. But by far the handsomest of them all
Was Aeneas, who came to her side now and joined
  forces with hers.
It was like when Apollo leaves Lycia, his winter
  palace,
And Xanthus river to visit Delos, his mother's home,
And renew the dances, while round his altar Cretans
  and Dryopes
And the tattooed Agathyrsi are raising a polyglot din:
The god himself steps out on the Cynthian range, a
  circlet
Of gold and a wreath of pliant bay on his flowing hair,
The jangling weapons slung from his shoulder. Nimble
  as he,
Aeneas moved, with the same fine glow on his
  handsome face.
When they had reached the mountains, the trackless
  haunt of game,
Wild goats – picture the scene! – started from crags up
  above there,
Ran down the slopes: from another direction stags
  were galloping
Over the open ground of a glen, deserting the heights –
A whole herd jostling together in flight, with a dust-
  cloud above it.
But young Ascanius, proud of his mettlesome horse,
  was riding
Along the vale, outstripping group after group of
  hunters,
And praying hard that, instead of such tame quarry, a
  frothing
Boar might come his way or a sand-coloured mountain
  lion.
At this stage a murmur, a growling began to be heard
In the sky: soon followed a deluge of rain and hail
  together.
The Trojan sportsmen, their Carthaginian friends and
  the grandson
Of Venus, in some alarm, scattered over the terrain
Looking for shelter. Torrents roared down from the
  mountain-tops.
Now Dido and the prince Aeneas found themselves
In the same cave. Primordial Earth and presiding Juno
Gave the signal. The firmament flickered with fire, a
  witness
Of wedding. Somewhere above, the Nymphs cried out
  in pleasure.
That day was doom's first birthday and that first day
  was the cause of
Evils: Dido recked nothing for appearance or

reputation:
The love she brooded on now was a secret love no
  longer;
Marriage, she called it, drawing the word to veil her
  sin.

Aeneid 4.259–86

As soon as his winged feet had carried him to the
  shacks there,
He noticed Aeneas superintending the work on towers
And new buildings: he wore a sword studded with
  yellow
Jaspers, and a fine cloak of glowing Tyrian purple
Hung from his shoulders – the wealthy Dido had
  fashioned it,
Interweaving the fabric with threads of gold, as a
  present to him.
Mercury went for him at once: So now you are laying
Foundations for lofty Carthage, building a beautiful
  city
To please a woman, lost to the interests of your own
  realm?
The king of the gods, who directs heaven and earth
  with his deity,
Sends me to you from bright Olympus: the king of the
  gods
Gave me this message to carry express through the air:
  What do you
Aim at or hope for, idling and fiddling here in Libya?
If you're indifferent to your own high destiny
And for your own renown you will make no effort at
  all,
Think of your young hopeful, Ascanius, growing to
  manhood,
The inheritance which you owe him – an Italian
  kingdom, the soil of
Rome. Such were the words which Mercury delivered;
And breaking off abruptly, was manifest no more,
But vanished into thin air, far beyond human ken.
Dazed indeed by that vision was Aeneas, and
  dumbfounded:
His hair stood on end with terror, the voice stuck in his
  throat.
Awed by his admonition from the great throne above,
He desired to fly the country, dear though it was to
  him.
But oh, what was he to do? What words could he find
  to get round
The temperamental queen? How broach the matter to
  her?
His mind was in feverish conflict, tossed from one side
  to the other,
Twisting and turning all ways to find a way past his
  dilemma.

Aeneid 4.305–30

Unfaithful man, did you think you could do such a
  dreadful thing
And keep it dark? yes, skulk from my land without one
  word?
Our love, the vows you made me – do these not give
  you pause,
Nor even the thought of Dido meeting a painful death?
Now, in the dead of winter, to be getting your ships
  ready
And hurrying to set sail when northerly gales are
  blowing,
You heartless one! Suppose the fields were not foreign,
  the home was
Not strange that you are bound for, suppose Troy stood
  as of old,
Would you be sailing for Troy, now, in this stormy
  weather?
Am I your reason for going? By these tears, by the
  hand you gave me –
They are all I have left, today, in my misery – I
  implore you,
And by our union of hearts, by our marriage hardly
  begun,
If I have ever helped you at all, if anything
About me pleased you, be sad for our broken home,
  forgo
Your purpose, I beg you, unless it's too late for prayers
  of mine! ...
If even I might have conceived a child by you before
You went away, a little Aeneas to play in the palace
And, in spite of all this, to remind me of you by his
  looks, oh then
I should not feel so utterly finished and desolate.

3 The death of Dido

Aeneid 4.331–61

She had spoken. Aeneas, mindful of Jove's words, kept
  his eyes
Unyielding, and with a great effort repressed his
  feeling for her.
In the end he managed to answer: – Dido, I'll never
  pretend
You have not been good to me, deserving of
  everything
You can claim. I shall not regret my memories of
  Elissa
As long as I breathe, as long as I remember my own
  self.
For my conduct – this, briefly: I did not look to make

off from here
In secret – do not suppose it; nor did I offer you
  marriage
At any time or consent to be bound by a marriage
  contract.
If fate allowed me to be my own master, and gave me
Free will to choose my way of life, to solve my
  problems,
Old Troy would be my first choice: I would restore it,
  and honour
My people's relics – the high walls of Priam
  perpetuated,
Troy given back to its conquered sons, a renaissant
  city,
Had been my task. But now Apollo and the Lycian
Oracle have told me that Italy is our bourne.
There lies my heart, my homeland. You, a Phoenician,
  are held by
These Carthaginian towers, by the charm of your
  Libyan city:
So can you grudge us Trojans our vision of settling
  down
In Italy? We too may seek a kingdom abroad.
Often as night envelops the earth in dewy darkness,
Often as star-rise, the troubled ghost of my father,
  Anchises,
Comes to me in my dreams, warns me and frightens
  me.
I am disturbed no less by the wrong I am doing
  Ascanius,
Defrauding him of his destined realm in Hesperia.
What's more, just now the courier of heaven, sent by
  Juppiter –
I swear it on your life and mine – conveyed to me,
  swiftly flying,
His orders: I saw the god, as clear as day, with my own
  eyes,
Entering the city, and these ears drank in the words he
  uttered.
No more reproaches, then – they only torture us both.
God's will, not mine, says 'Italy'.

Aeneid 4.393–415

But the god-fearing Aeneas, much as he longed to
  soothe
Her anguish with consolation, with words that would
  end her troubles,
Heavily sighing, his heart melting from love of her,
Nevertheless obeyed the gods and went off to his fleet.
Whereupon the Trojans redoubled their efforts, all
  along
The beach dragging down the tall ships, launching the
  well-tarred bottoms,

Fetching green wood to make oars, and baulks of
    unfashioned timber
From the forest, so eager they were to be gone.
You could see them on the move, hurrying out of the
    city.
It looked like an army of ants when, provident for
    winter,
They're looting a great big corn-heap and storing it up
    in their own house;
Over a field the black file goes, as they carry the loot
On a narrow track through the grass; some are
    strenuously pushing
The enormous grains of corn with their shoulders,
    while others marshal
The traffic and keep it moving: their whole road
    seethes with activity.
Ah, Dido, what did you feel when you saw these things
    going forward?
What moans you gave when, looking forth from your
    high roof-top,
You beheld the whole length of the beach aswarm with
    men, and the sea's face
Alive with the sound and fury of preparations for
    sailing!
Excess of love, to what lengths you drive our human
    hearts!
Once again she was driven to try what tears and
    entreaties
Could do, and let love beggar her pride – she would
    leave no appeal
Untried, lest, for want of it, she should all needlessly
    die.

Aeneid 4.607–29

O sun, with your beams surveying all that is done on
    earth!
Juno, the mediator and witness of my tragedy!
Hecate, whose name is howled by night at the city
    crossroads!
Avenging Furies, and you, the patrons of dying
    Elissa! –
Hear me! Incline your godheads to note this
    wickedness
So worthy of your wrath! And hear my prayer! If he,
That damned soul, must make port and get to land, if
    thus
Jove destines it, if that bourne is fixed for him
    irrevocably,
May he be harried in war by adventurous tribes, and
    exiled
From his own land; may Ascanius to be torn from his
    arms; may he have to
Sue for aid, and see his own friends squalidly dying.
Yes, and when he's accepted the terms of a harsh

peace,
Let him never enjoy his realm or the allotted span,
But fall before his time and lie on the sands, unburied.
That is my last prayer. I pour it out, with my lifeblood.
Let you, my Tyrians, sharpen your hatred upon his
    children
And all their seed for ever: send this as a present to
My ghost. Between my people and his, no love, no
    alliance!
Rise up from my dead bones, avenger! Rise up, one
To hound the Trojan settlers with fire and steel
    remorselessly,
Now, some day, whenever the strength for it shall be
    granted!
Shore to shore, sea to sea, weapon to weapon
    opposed –
I call down a feud between them and us to the last
    generation!

Aeneid 4.642–71

But Dido, trembling, distraught by the terrible things
    she was doing,
Her bloodshot eyes all restless, with hectic blotches
    upon
Her quivering cheeks, yet pale with the shade of
    advancing death,
Ran to the innermost court of the palace, climbed the
    lofty
Pyre, frantic at heart, and drew Aeneas' sword –
Her present to him, procured once for a far different
    purpose.
Then, after eyeing the clothes he had left behind, the
    memoried
Bed, pausing to weep and brood on him for a little,
She lay down on the bed and spoke her very last
    words: –
O relics of him, things dear to me while fate, while
    heaven allowed,
Receive this life of mine, release me from my troubles!
I have lived, I have run to the finish the course which
    fortune gave me:
And now, a queenly shade, I shall pass to the world
    below.
I built a famous city, saw my own place established,
Avenged a husband, exacted a price for a brother's
    enmity.
Happy I would have been, ah, beyond words happy,
If only the Trojan ships had never come to my shore!
These words; then, burying her face in the bed: – Shall
    I die unavenged?
At least, let me die. Thus, thus! I go to the dark, go
    gladly.
May he look long, from out there on the deep, at my
    flaming pyre.

The heartless! And may my death-fires signal bad luck
for his voyage!
She had spoken; and with these words, her attendants
saw her falling
Upon the sword, they could see the blood spouting up
over
The blade, and her hands spattered. Their screams rang
to the roofs of
The palace; then rumour ran amok through the shocked
city.
All was weeping and wailing, the streets were filled
with a keening
Of women, the air resounded with terrible
lamentations.
It was as if Carthage or ancient Tyre should be falling,
With enemy troops breaking into the town and a
conflagration
Furiously sweeping over the abodes of men and of
gods.

Aeneid 4.672–705

Anna heard it: half dead from extreme fear, she ran
through
The crowd, tearing her cheeks with her nails, beating
her breast
With her fists, and called aloud by name on the dying
woman: –
So this was your purpose, Dido? You were making a
dupe of me?
That pyre, those lighted altars – for me, they were
leading to this?
How shall I chide you for leaving me? Were you too
proud to let your
Sister die with you? You should have called me to
share your end:
One hour, one pang of the sword could have carried us
both away.
Did I build this pyre with my own hands, invoking our
family gods,
So that you might lie on it, and I, the cause of your
troubles, not be there?
You have destroyed more than your self – me, and the
lords
And commons and city of Sidon. Quick! Water for her
wounds!
Let me bathe them, and if any last breath is fluttering
from her mouth,
Catch it in mine! So saying, she had scaled the
towering pyre,
Taken the dying woman into her lap, was caressing her,
Sobbing, trying to staunch the dark blood with her own
dress.
Dido made an effort to raise her heavy eyes,
Then gave it up: the sword-blade grated against her

breast bone.
Three times she struggled to rise, to lift herself on an
elbow,
Three times rolled back on the bed. Her wandering
gaze went up
To the sky, looking for light: she gave a moan when
she saw it.
Then did almighty Juno take pity on her long-drawn-
out
Sufferings and hard going, sent Iris down from
Olympus
To part the agonized soul from the body that still clung
to it.
Since she was dying neither a natural death nor from
others'
Violence, but desperate and untimely, driven to it
By a crazed impulse, not yet had Proserpine clipped
from her head
The golden tress, or consigned her soul to the
Underworld.
So now, all dewy, her pinions the colour of yellow
crocus,
Her wake a thousand rainbow hues refracting the
sunlight,
Iris flew down, and over Dido hovering, said: –
As I was bidden, I take this sacred thing, the Death-
god's
Due: and you I release from your body. She snipped
the tress.
Then all warmth went at once, the life was lost in air.

Livy

1 Hannibal prepares to invade Italy

21.1.1–3

I may well, at this point, declare that I am now about to
tell the story of the most memorable war in history:
that, namely, which was fought by Carthage under the
leadership of Hannibal against Rome. It was fought
between peoples unrivalled throughout previous history
in material resources, and themselves at the peak of
their prosperity and power; secondly, it was a struggle
between old antagonists, each of whom had learned, in
the first Punic War, to appreciate the military
capabilities of the other; thirdly, the final issue hung so
much in doubt that the eventual victors came nearer to
destruction than their adversaries. Moreover, mutual
hatred was hardly less sharp a weapon than the sword;
on the Roman side there was rage at the unprovoked
attack by a previously beaten enemy; on the

Carthaginian, bitter resentment at what was felt to be the grasping and tyrannical attitude of their conquerors.

21.1.4, 2.3

An anecdote of Hannibal's boyhood: his father Hamilcar, after the campaign in Africa, was about to carry his troops over into Spain, when Hannibal, then about nine years old, begged, with all the childish arts he could muster, to be allowed to accompany him; whereupon Hamilcar, who was preparing to offer sacrifice, led the boy to the altar and made him solemnly swear, with his hand upon the sacred victim, that as soon as he was old enough he would be the enemy of the Roman people.

That the war was postponed was due to Hamilcar's timely death and the fact that Hannibal was still too young to assume command. The interval between father and son was filled by Hasdrubal, who commanded the Carthaginian armies for some eight years.

21.4

Hannibal was sent to Spain, where the troops received him with unanimous enthusiasm, the old soldiers feeling that in the person of this young man Hamilcar himself was restored to them. In the features and expression of the son's face they saw the father once again, the same vigour in his look, the same fire in his eyes. Very soon he no longer needed to rely upon his father's memory to make himself beloved and obeyed: his own qualities were sufficient.

Power to command and readiness to obey are rare associates; but in Hannibal they were perfectly united, and their union made him as much valued by his commander as by his men. Hasdrubal preferred him to all other officers in any action which called for vigour and courage, and under his leadership the men invariably showed to the best advantage both dash and confidence. Reckless in courting danger, he showed superb tactical ability once it was upon him. Indefatigable both physically and mentally, he could endure with equal ease excessive heat or excessive cold; he ate and drank not to flatter his appetites but only so much as would sustain his bodily strength. His time for waking, like his time for sleeping, was never determined by daylight or darkness. Often he was seen lying in his cloak on the bare ground amongst the common soldiers on sentry or picket duty. Mounted or unmounted he was unequalled as a fighting man, always the first to attack, the last to leave the field.

So much for his virtues – and they were great; but no less great were his faults: inhuman cruelty, a more than Punic perfidy, a total disregard of truth, honour, and religion, of the sanctity of an oath and of all that

other men hold sacred. Such was the complex character of the man who for three years served under Hasdrubal's command, doing and seeing everything which could help to equip him as a great military leader.

21.21.1–8

After the capture of Saguntum Hannibal had retired to winter quarters in New Carthage. News was brought him of the various activities in Rome and Carthage and of the decisions which had been made, so when he learned that he was himself the cause of the coming war as well as the commander-in-chief of the Carthaginian armies, he determined to act swiftly. As soon as he had completed the division and sale of the remainder of the captured material, he summoned a meeting of his Spanish troops, and addressed them as follows:

'My friends, no doubt you see as well as I do that, with all the Spanish peoples subject to our influence, one of two courses is open to us: either we must stop fighting and disband our armies, or pursue our conquests elsewhere. Since, therefore, we are soon to fight a campaign in distant parts and nobody knows when you may see your homes and loved ones again, I have decided to grant leave of absence to any man who wishes to visit his family. Your orders are to return to duty at the beginning of spring, in order that, with God's help, we may begin a war which will fill your pockets with gold and carry your fame to the world's end.' For most of the men the unexpected offer of leave was very welcome. The whole winter was a time of inactivity between two periods of hard service, one completed, the other still to be faced, and the respite gave the troops fresh strength, both physical and moral, to endure again all that might be required of them. At the beginning of spring they reassembled according to orders.

21.27.1–8, 28.1–4

As soon as preparations were complete, they were deterred from proceeding by an assembly in force of the enemy, both horse and foot, who were thronging the farther bank of the river. To circumvent this menace, Hannibal sent Hanno with a party of men, mostly Spanish, a day's journey up the river; his instructions were to start soon after dark and, on the first opportunity, to cross over, attracting as little attention as possible, and then, by an outflanking movement, to attack the enemy in the rear. Information was given by the Gallic guides that some twenty-five miles upstream there was a convenient place for crossing, where the river was broader and shallower as it was split into two channels by a small island.

Timber was quickly cut and rafts constructed to

carry the men over, together with their horses and gear, the Spanish troops making no bones about swimming across. The rest of the force crossed on the rafts, lashed together to form a bridge. Camp was then pitched near the river bank, and the men were given a day's rest to recover from their night march and subsequent labours, their commanding officer being anxious to avoid any sort of miscarriage in the operation. Next day they got on the move again, and raised a smoke signal to indicate that they were across the river and not far away. Hannibal saw the signal, and gave immediate orders for his own men to begin their passage of the river, a line of larger craft being stationed just above them to break the force of the current, and to make easier going for the rafts and boats farther downstream. The Gallic warriors came surging to the river bank, howling and singing as their custom was, shaking their shields above their heads and brandishing their spears, in spite of the menace which confronted them of those innumerable hostile craft, rendered yet more alarming by the roar of the stream and the cries of the soldiers and sailors struggling to overcome the fierce current and the shouts of encouragement from their comrades awaiting their turn to cross.

All this was bad enough; but suddenly, from behind, a more terrible sound assailed their ears – the triumphant shout of Hanno's men. Their camp had been captured, and a moment later Hanno himself was upon them: they were caught between two deadly menaces, the thousands of armed men landing on the river bank and a second army unexpectedly pressing upon their rear. After one fruitless attempt at active resistance they forced a way out of the trap as best they could and dispersed in confusion to their villages. Hannibal, now convinced that there was more smoke than fire in Gallic resistance, completed at leisure the passage of the river, and pitched camp.

2 Hannibal reaches the Alps

21.32.6–7

From the Druentia Hannibal advanced towards the Alps mainly through open country, and reached the foothills without encountering any opposition from the local tribes. The dreadful vision was now before their eyes: the towering peaks, the snow-clad pinnacles soaring to the sky, the rude huts clinging to the rocks, beasts and cattle shrivelled and parched with cold, the people with their wild and ragged hair, all nature, animate and inanimate, stiff with frost: all this gave a fresh edge to their apprehension.

21.32.8–10

As the column moved forward up the first slopes, there appeared, right above their heads, ensconced upon their eminences, the local tribesmen, wild men of the mountains, who, if they had chosen to lurk in clefts of the hills, might well have sprung out from ambush upon the marching column and inflicted untold losses and disaster.

Hannibal soon ordered a halt and sent his Gallic guides forward to reconnoitre. Informed that he could not get through there, he encamped in the best stretch of fairly level ground he could find. Later he learned from the same guides, whose way of life and language were much like those of the local tribesmen, and who had been able, in consequence, to listen to their deliberations, that the pass was held only in the daytime, and that at nightfall the natives dispersed to their homes. In view of this information, at dawn next morning he approached the eminences where the tribesmen were on watch as if with the intention of openly trying to force a passage through the defile during the hours of daylight.

21.32.11–33.4

During the rest of the day he concealed his actual purpose; his men fortified the position where they had originally halted, and it was not till he was sure that the tribesmen had abandoned the heights and gone off guard that his real intention became evident. Leaving the baggage in camp with all the cavalry and most of the infantry, and kindling, for a blind, more fires than the numbers actually left in camp would justify, he assembled a force of light-armed infantrymen, swiftly cleared the defile, and established himself on the heights which the tribesmen had been holding.

At dawn next morning camp was broken up and the rest of the army moved forward. The tribesmen were beginning to muster at their usual look-out station on the heights when, to their astonishment, they saw the Carthaginian assault-troops right above their heads and already in possession of it, while another army of them was passing through along the track. The two things together were such a shock to them that for the moment they were frozen into immobility; soon, however, the sight of the enemy's own difficulties restored their confidence. In the narrow pass the marching column was rapidly losing cohesion; so the tribesmen, in the hope that any hostile action by themselves would be enough to complete their discomfiture, came swarming down the rocky and precipitous slopes.

21.33.5–11

The Carthaginians thus found themselves facing two enemies – the hostile tribesmen and the terrible difficulty of their position in the narrow defile. It was a case of every man for himself, and in their struggles to get clear of danger they were fighting with each other rather than with the enemy. It was the horses, more than anything else, which created havoc in the column: terrified by the din, echoing and re-echoing from the hollow cliffs and woods, they were soon out of control, while those which were struck or wounded lashed out in an agony of fear, causing serious losses both of men and gear of all descriptions. In the confusion many were flung over the sheer cliffs which bounded each side of the pass, and fell to their deaths thousands of feet below; but it was worst for the pack-animals – loads and all, they went tumbling over the edge almost like falling masonry.

All this was a shocking spectacle; nevertheless Hannibal, watching from above, stayed for the moment where he was and kept his assault-troops in check, lest their joining the column should only add to the confusion. But when he saw the column break up, hurrying down from his position on the heights, he scattered the hostile tribesmen with a single charge. His arrival did, indeed, increase the confusion amongst his own men, but only for a moment; for once the enemy had fled and the track was clear, order was restored, and it was not long before the whole army, unmolested and almost in silence, was brought safely through.

The chief fortified village of the district, together with the neighbouring hamlets, was then captured, and the cattle and grain taken from these places proved sufficient to feed the army for three days. As the tribesmen had learnt their lesson, and the going was now comparatively easy, the army during these three days made considerable progress.

21.34–35.3

Coming to the territory of another mountain tribe, a numerous one for this sort of country, Hannibal encountered no open resistance, but fell into a cunningly laid trap. In fact he nearly succumbed to the very tactics in which he himself excelled. The elders of the fortified villages presented themselves in the guise of envoys, and declared that the wholesome example of others' suffering had taught them to prefer the friendship of the Carthaginians to the risk of learning at first hand of their military might. They were willing, in consequence, to submit to Hannibal's orders, to supply him with guides and provisions, and to offer hostages as a guarantee of their good faith.

Hannibal was too cautious to take what they said at its face value, but was unwilling to reject the offer out of hand, lest a refusal should drive them into open hostility; accordingly he replied in friendly terms, accepted the hostages, and made use of the supplies the natives had offered; he then followed their guides – by no means proceeding in loose order. At the head of the column were the cavalry and elephants; Hannibal himself, with the pick of the infantry, brought up the rear, keeping his eyes open and alert for every contingency.

Before long the column found itself on a narrowing track, one side of which was overhung by a precipitous wall of rock, and it was suddenly attacked. The natives, springing from their places of concealment, fiercely assaulted front and rear, leaping into the fray, hurling missiles, rolling down rocks from the heights above. The worst pressure was on Hannibal's rear; even as it was the moment was critical, and disaster only just averted; for Hannibal hesitated to send his own division into the pass and his hesitation enabled the tribesmen to deliver a flank attack, cut the whole column in two, and establish themselves on the track. As a result, Hannibal, for one night, found himself cut off from his cavalry and baggage-train.

Next day, however, as enemy activity weakened, a junction was effected between the two halves of the column and the defile was successfully passed, though not without losses, especially amongst the pack-animals. Thenceforward there was no concerted opposition, the natives confining themselves to mere raids, in small parties, on front or rear, as the nature of the ground dictated, or as groups of stragglers, left behind or pressing on ahead of the column as the case might be, offered a tempting prey. The elephants proved both a blessing and a curse: for though getting them along the narrow tracks caused serious delay, they were none the less a protection to the troops, as the natives, never having seen such creatures before, were afraid to come near them.

3 Hannibal crosses the Alps

21.35.4–9

On the ninth day the army reached the summit. Most of the climb had been over trackless mountain-sides; frequently a wrong route was taken – sometimes through the deliberate deception of the guides, or, again, when some likely-looking valley would be entered by guess-work, without knowledge of whither it led. There was a two days' halt on the summit, to rest the men after the exhausting climb and the fighting. Some of the pack-animals which had fallen amongst the rocks managed, by following the army's tracks, to find their way into camp.

The troops had indeed endured hardships enough; but there was worse to come. It began to snow. Getting on the move at dawn, the army struggled slowly forward over snow-covered ground, the hopelessness of utter exhaustion in every face. Seeing their despair, Hannibal rode ahead and at a point of vantage which afforded a prospect of a vast extent of country, he gave the order to halt, pointing to Italy far below, and the Po Valley beyond the foothills of the Alps. 'My men,' he said 'you are at this moment passing the protective barrier of Italy – nay more, you are walking over the very walls of Rome. Henceforward all will be easy going – no more hills to climb. After a fight or two you will have the capital of Italy, the citadel of Rome, in the hollow of your hands.'

21.35.10–36.4

The march continued, more or less without molestation from the natives, who confined themselves to petty raids when they saw a chance of stealing something. Unfortunately, however, as in most parts of the Alps the descent on the Italian side, being shorter, is correspondingly steeper, the going was much more difficult than it had been during the ascent. The track was almost everywhere precipitous, narrow, and slippery; it was impossible for a man to keep his feet; the least stumble meant a fall, and a fall a slide, so that there was indescribable confusion, men and beasts stumbling and slipping on top of each other.

Soon they found themselves on the edge of a precipice – a narrow cliff falling away so sheer that even a light-armed soldier could hardly have got down it by feeling his way and clinging to such bushes and stumps as presented themselves. It must always have been a most awkward spot, but a recent landslide had converted it on this occasion to a perpendicular drop of nearly a thousand feet. On the brink the cavalry drew rein – their journey seemed to be over. Hannibal, in the rear, did not yet know what had brought the column to a halt; but when the message was passed to him that there was no possibility of proceeding, he went in person to reconnoitre. It was clear to him that a detour would have to be made, however long it might prove to be, over the trackless and untrodden slopes in the vicinity.

21.37.1–3

When it became apparent that both men and beasts were wearing themselves out to no purpose, a space was cleared – with the greatest labour because of the amount of snow to be dug and carted away – and camp was pitched, high up on the ridge. The next task was to construct some sort of passable track down the precipice, for by no other route could the army proceed. It was necessary to cut through rock; large trees were felled and lopped, and a huge pile of timber erected; this, with the opportune help of a strong wind, was set on fire, and when the rock was sufficiently heated the men's rations of sour wine were flung upon it, to render it friable. They then got to work with picks on the heated rock, and opened a sort of zigzag track, to minimize the steepness of the descent, and were able, in consequence, to get the pack animals, and even the elephants, down it.

21.37.4–38.1

Four days were spent in the neighbourhood of this precipice; the animals came near to dying of starvation, for on most of the peaks nothing grows, or, if there is any pasture, the snow covers it. Lower down there are sunny hills and valleys and woods with streams flowing by: country, in fact, more worthy for men to dwell in. There the beasts were put out to pasture, and the troops given three days' rest to recover from the fatigue of their road-building. Thence the descent was continued to the plains – a kindlier region, with kindlier inhabitants.

The march to Italy was much as I have described it.

39.51

The legate Titus Quinctius Flamininus came to King Prusias. There because Prusias himself – so that he might do a favour to Flamininus, who was on the spot, and to the Romans – conceived a plan of taking the initiative and killing or handing him (Hannibal) into their power, as a result of his first conversation with Flamininus soldiers were immediately sent to guard Hannibal's house.

Hannibal had always foreseen such an end to his life, both because he saw the implacable hatred of the Romans against himself and because he put no faith at all in the trustworthiness of kings; indeed he had even had experience of the unreliability of Prusias; he had also felt fear at the arrival of Flamininus as if it would prove fatal to him. In the face of all the dangers which surrounded him, so that he could always have some route available for escape, he had made seven exits from his house, some of them secret so that they could not be blocked off by guards.

But they (the king's men) so (effectively) surrounded the perimeter of the whole house with guards that nobody could slip out from there. After it was announced that the king's soldiers were in the entrance-court, Hannibal tried to flee by the back door, which was the most secret. When he realized that this also was blocked off by the soldiers stationed there and that everywhere round about was fenced in by the guards positioned there, he demanded the poison which he had with him for a long time before this ready for such emergencies, and said, 'Let us free the Roman people from their long-lasting anxiety, since they consider it a long business to wait for the death of an old man. It will be no great or memorable victory that Flamininus will win from an unarmed victim of betrayal.'

Then having cursed the life and kingdom of Prusias and calling upon the gods of hospitality as witnesses of the pledge he had abused, he drained the draught. This was the way in which Hannibal ended his life.

Juvenal: *Satires* 10.147–67

Weigh Hannibal: how many pounds will you find in
    that mighty
commander? This is the man too big for Africa – a
    land
which is pounded by the Moorish sea and extends to
    the steaming Nile.
He annexes Spain to his empire, and dances lightly
    across
the Pyrenees; then nature bars his path with the snowy
    Alps;
by vinegar's aid he splits the rocks and shatters the
    mountains.
Italy now is within his grasp; but he still presses on.
'Nought is achieved,' he cries, 'until I have smashed
    the gates
with my Punic troops, and raised our flag in the central
    Subura!'
Lord, what a sight! It would surely have made an
    amazing picture:
the one-eyed general riding on his huge Gaetulian
    beast.
So how does the story end? Alas for glory! Our hero
is beaten. He scrambles away into exile, and there he
    sits
in the hall of the monarch's palace, a great and
    conspicuous client,
until it shall please his Bithynian lord to greet the day.
That soul which once convulsed the world will meet its
    end,
not from a sword, or stones, or spears, but from an
    object
which, avenging Cannae, will take reprisal for all that
    bloodshed –
a ring. Go on, you maniac; charge through the Alpine
    wastes
to entertain a class of boys and become an oration!

Ovid

1 Ovid tells the story of his life

Tristia 4.10 (with omissions)

I, whom you read, I, fond love's witty poet,
    Learn who I was, you of the years to come.
My home is Sulmo, rich in ice-cold waters,
    A town that's distant ninety miles from Rome.
There I was born, the day on which both consuls
    Met death together, if you'd know the date.
I was not first; my birth followed my brother's;
    He came before me, just twelve months away.
The same day-star attended both our birthdays:
    Two cakes to celebrate a single day.

As young lads we were trained; our father sent us
    To men distinguished in the arts at Rome.
From his green years my brother's bent was
               eloquence;
    In the court's war of words he was at home.
But I, while still a boy, loved Heaven's service;
    The Muse enticed me to her task by stealth.
My father often said, 'Why try a useless
    Vocation? Even Homer left no wealth.'
So I obeyed, all Helicon abandoned,
    And tried to write in prose that did not scan.
But poetry in metre came unbidden,
    And what I tried to write in verses ran.

Meanwhile, as silent years slipped by, the toga
    Of adult freedom we two brothers wore,
With, on our shoulders, the broad stripe of purple,
    And our pursuits continued as before.
And now my brother, at the age of twenty,
    Died and I learnt the loss of part of me.
I held awhile a young man's first appointment
    And was one member of the Board of Three.

Then there remained the Senate, but I narrowed
    My stripe: beyond my strength the load would be,
Body and mind alike unfit for labour,
    Ambition and its worries not for me.
The Muses too were urging me to follow
    My true love, leisure in serenity.

The poets of those days I loved and honoured,
    Each of those bards a god in my belief.
Propertius would recite his fiery lyrics,
    So close a comradeship linked him and me,
Horace too, master-metrist, charmed me, singing
    His polished stanzas to the Latin lyre.
Virgil I only saw, and with Tibullus
    Friendship was thwarted by Fate's greedy pyre.

As I those elders honoured, so the younger
    Me, nor was my Muse slow in finding fame.
When I first read my youthful verse in public,
    My beard had only once or twice been trimmed.
My talent had been kindled by Corinna
    (Not her real name), throughout the city hymned.
My heart was soft, no match for Cupid's weapons,
    A heart the slightest spark would set aflame.
Yet, though the least thing moved me – such my
                                                nature –
    No breath of scandal ever touched my name.

My head was hoar, my better years behind me,
    My ancient tresses blending white with grey,
When the hurt prince's rage forced me to Tomis
    Far on the left shore of the Euxine Sea.

Tristia 1.3 (with omissions)

When in my thoughts that tragic night is pictured
    Which in the City formed my final hour,
That night on which I left so much I treasured,
    Now once again from my sad eyes tears shower.
The dawn was near on which by Caesar's order
    From Italy's last bounds I must depart.
No more delay! My mind was numb: for proper
    Arrangements I had neither time nor heart.
No thought of choosing slaves or a companion,
    No kit or clothes an exile ought to wear.
I was as stunned as someone struck by lightning,
    Who lives, yet of his life is unaware.

But when my pain itself cleared my mind's
                                                stormcloud,
    And senses in the end some strength regained,
I spoke to my sad friends last words of parting:
    So many once – now one or two remained.
I was in tears. My wife, in tears more bitter,
    Held me, her blameless cheeks wet endlessly.
My daughter, far away on shores of Libya,
    Could not be told the fate befallen me.
Look where you might, it seemed a noisy funeral;
    You heard the sounds of grief and sorrow swell
Inside the house …

Ah, then, as I was leaving, my wife hugged me
    And mingled with my tears her words of woe:
'We can't be parted. We shall go together:
    An exiled wife, I'll share an exile's fate.
You Caesar's wrath compels to leave our country,
    Me, love. For me that love shall Caesar be.'
She tried, as she had tried before, and hardly
    Surrendered, yielding to expediency.

2 Ovid the lover

Amores 2.6 (with omissions)

Her parrot, flying mimic from the Indies,
    Is dead. Come, every bird, come flocking round,
Beat wings on breasts, tear tender cheeks with talons,
    All at her obsequies, in duty bound;
Mourn, every bird that in the bright air poises,
    But chiefly you his friend, the turtle-dove.
Your whole lives passed in harmony together,
    And steadfast to the end your loyal love.
But what avail were loyalty, rare colours,
    Your voice's brilliant gift of mimicry,
The joy that from the first you gave my darling?
    Glory of birds, poor parrot, dead you lie.
He's died, that mimic of our human voices,
    The parrot, gift that came from the world's end.
The seventh dawn could find no dawn to follow,
    'Farewell, Corinna' was its dying cry.

Amores 1.5 (with omissions)

(Marlowe's version, slightly modernized)

    In summer's heat and mid-time of the day
    To rest my limbs upon a bed I lay.
    One shutter closed, the other open stood,
    Which gave such light as lies within a wood,
    Like twilight shade at setting of the sun,
    Or when night's gone and yet day not begun.
    Such light for bashful girls one should provide,
    In which their shyness may have hope to hide.

    In came Corinna in a long loose gown,
    Her white neck hid with tresses hanging down;
    I snatched her gown; being thin the harm was small,
    Yet strove she to be covered therewithal,
    And striving thus as one who wished to fail,
    Was simply beaten by her self-betrayal.
    Stark naked as she stood before mine eye,
    No blemish on her body could I spy.
    What arms and shoulders did I touch and see,
    How apt her bosom to be pressed by me!
    Belly so smooth below the breasts so high,
    And waist so long, and what a fine young thigh.
    Why detail more? All perfect in my sight;
    And naked as she was, I hugged her tight.
    And next – all know! We rested, with a kiss;
    Jove send me more such afternoons as this!

Ars Amatoria 1.89–132 (with omissions)

But the tiered playhouse gives you amplest scope;
There's hunting richer than you dared to hope.
There you shall find a mistress or a toy
To touch but once or be a lasting joy.
As ants that to and fro in endless train
Haste to bring home their wonted load of grain,
As mid their favourite glades and scented leas
O'er flowers and thyme-tops flit the swarming bees,
So to the play the well-dressed bevies throng,
Such wealth of choice as keeps one doubting long.
They come to look and to be looked at too.
Ah! Virtue, it's a fatal spot for you.

With Romulus the scandal first began,
When ravished Sabines cheered his wifeless clan.
On tiers of terraced turf the folk reclined,
Rough crowns of leaves their shaggy hair entwined.
They look, and each one marks his chosen fair,
Each in his heart breathes many a silent prayer.

Amid the applause (applause was natural then)
The chieftain signals on his waiting men.
Up suddenly with tell-tale shouts they spring,
And hungry hands upon the maidens fling.
As frightened doves before the eagle fly,
As lambkins that the dreaded wolf espy,
So they before the men's wild onset shrink,
And not a cheek retains its wonted pink.

All fear alike, but fear has many a phase;
Some rend their hair, some sit in lost amaze,
One mutely mourns, one vainly 'Mother' cries,
One sobs, one faints, one stays, another flies.
And if one strove her captor to deny,
Clasped to his loving breast he held her high:
'Why spoil those tender eyes with tears?' quoth he,
'Just like your parents you and I shall be.'
Old Romulus the prize for soldiers knew,
For such a prize I'd be a soldier too!

Amores 3.2 (with omissions)

I don't sit here because I'm keen on bloodstock,
    Though may the horse you've backed the winner be.
I came to talk with you, to sit beside you,
    So that you'll learn the love you've lit in me.
You watch the course, and I watch you; together
    Let's both watch what we want and feast our eyes.
Happy the charioteer who's found your favour!
    That fellow's got the luck; it's him you prize.

I wish that luck was mine. I'd get the horses
    Galloping from the start, I'd be so brave;

I'd give them rein, I'd use my whip, as need be,
    And with my nearside wheel the post I'd shave;
But seeing you as I swept by I'd falter,
    My hands would drop the reins and loose they'd lie.

Why edge away? It's no use; the line keeps us
    Close – one good thing about the seating here.
You on the right there, careful, please. You're hurting
    The lady with your elbow; you're too near.
And you on the seat behind us, draw your legs back,
    And mind your manners. Keep your hard knees
                                        clear.

They've cleared the course – the great event – the
                                        praetor's
    Started the four-horse chariots. Off they go!
That's yours. The one you back will be the winner;
    Your wishes even the horses seem to know.
Oh, Hell! What is he at? The fellow's taken
    The post too wide. They're neck and neck again.
What are you at, you idiot? You're wrecking
    The girl's best hopes. Left rein! Hard now, left rein!

We've backed a snail. Recall them, give the signal,
    Good Romans! Wave your togas everywhere!
Look, they're recalled. My cloak can give you shelter,
    So waving togas won't disturb your hair.
And now again the starting-gates are open,
    All those bright colours galloping away.
Come on now, take the lead down those wide furlongs,
    And make her hopes and mine come true today.
My girl's hopes have come true; my hopes are
                                        waiting.
    He's won his palm; my palm is still to wear.
She smiled; those bright eyes surely promised
                                        something.
    Enough for here. Give me the rest elsewhere.

Metamorphoses 8.618–94 (with omissions)

'The power of heaven is great and has no bounds;
Whatever the gods determine is fulfilled.
I give you proof. Among the Phrygian hills
An oak tree and a lime grow side by side,
Girt by a little wall. I saw the place
With my own eyes …
Not far from these two trees there is a marsh,
Once habitable land, but water now,
The busy home of divers, duck and coot.
Here once came Jupiter, in mortal guise,
And with his father herald Mercury,
His wings now laid aside. A thousand homes
They came to seeking rest; a thousand homes
Were barred against them; yet one welcomed them,

Tiny indeed, and thatched with reeds and straw;
But in that cottage Baucis, old and good,
And old Philemon (he as old as she)
Had joined their lives in youth, grown old together,
And eased their poverty by bearing it
Contentedly and thinking it no shame.
It was vain to seek master and servant there;
They two were all the household, to obey
And to command. So when the heavenly ones
Reached their small home and, stooping, entered in
At the low door, the old man placed a bench
And bade them sit and rest their weary limbs.

Meanwhile they saw, when the wine-bowl was
    drained,
Each time it filled itself, and wine welled up
All of its own accord within the bowl.
In fear and wonder Baucis and Philemon,
With hands upturned, joined in a timid prayer
And pardon sought for the crude graceless meal.
There was one goose, the trusty guardian
Of their minute domain and they, the hosts,
Would sacrifice him for the Gods, their guests.
But he, swift-winged, wore out their slow old bones
And long escaped them, till at last he seemed
To flee for sanctuary to the Gods themselves.
The deities forbade. 'We too are gods,'
They said; 'This wicked neighbourhood shall pay
Just punishment; but to you there shall be given
Exemption from this evil. Leave your home,
Accompany our steps and climb with us
The mountain slopes.' The two old folk obey
And slowly struggle up the long ascent,
Propped on their sticks.

3 Ovid in exile

Tristia 1.2 (with omissions)

O gods of sea and sky – for what is left now
    But prayer? – let not our ship, caught in the gale,
Be shattered …
Ay me! What mountain crests of seas are rolling!
    The stars above you'd think they're touching now.
What yawning valleys sink when waves are sundered!
    You'd think they're touching now black Hell below.
Gaze as I may – nothing but sky and ocean,
    Clouds threaten there and here wild billows swell.
Between them monstrous winds are madly roaring;
    Which master to obey the waves can't tell.
The helmsman doubts what course to shun or follow,
    The baffling perils paralyse his skill.
The breakers swamp my face as I am speaking;
    No hope at all of safety: die we will.

Tristia 3.10 (with omissions)

If someone there remembers banished Ovid
    And in the City my name without me
Lives, let him know I dwell among barbarians
    Beneath the stars that never touch the sea,
Sauromatae, fierce race, Bessi and Getae,
    Names how unworthy of my genius!
Yet while the breeze is warm the severing Danube
    Is our defence; his waves keep war from us.

But when grim winter rears its murky visage
    And white with ice like marble the land lies,
Snow lies and, as it lies, no sun or rain can
    Melt it, congealed for ever by the wind.
When the North wind is roused its onslaught levels
    Towers to the ground and roofs away are reft.
They keep the cold at bay with skins and breeches;
    Of the whole body just the face is left.
With icicles the hair will often tinkle
    And beards are white with frost below the lips.

Why tell of rivers icy cold has conquered,
    And splitting water hacked from lakes and meres?
Where boats went, now they go on foot, and hooves of
    Horses pound currents that the cold congeals.
I've seen the vast sea solid ice, the water
    Becalmed below a slippery carapace.
Ships will stand clamped in ice as though in marble;
    The rigid water oars can never rive;
And in the ice I've seen fish stuck and fastened,
    Yet even then a few were still alive.

As soon as its [the North wind's] dry blasts have
                        planed the Danube,
    With swift steeds comes the barbarous enemy.
They come with might of steeds and far-shot arrows
    And far and wide the neighbourhood's their prey.
Some flee and, when none stay to guard the
                        farmsteads,
    Their unprotected wealth is swept away.
Some too are captured and, arms bound behind them,
    In vain on homes and fields they turn their eyes.
Some die in torment, victims of barbed arrows;
    No flying point its prime of poison lacks.
The hordes destroy what they can't drive or carry,
    And flames consume the unoffending shacks.

Still, when peace comes, the dread of war distresses
    And no man to the plough will put his hand.
This place sees foes or, when not seen, it fears them;
    Abandoned, hard and idle, lies the land.
No tree, no leaf! The fields he'd see lie naked,
    A place where no man not ill-starred should be!
So this, although the great globe spreads so broadly,
    This is the land that's found to punish me!

Tristia 3.3 (with omissions)

If you should wonder why my letter's written
    By another hand, I have been ill; I've lain
Ill in an unknown world's remotest regions,
    Doubting indeed if I'd be well again.
I can't endure the climate or get used to
    The water and the soil's upsetting me.
There's no fit house or food to help in sickness,
    No doctor's skill to ease my aching woe,
No friend to comfort or with conversation
    Beguile the hours that creep along so slow.
As I lie tired among these farthest peoples,
    My sick brain thinks of all that is not here.
In all those thoughts the thought of you is foremost;
    The first place in my heart is yours, my dear.
You, far away, I talk to; your name only
    I speak; without you comes no night, no day.

And greeting him, their young brows wreathed with bay,
    Come Calvus and Catullus …
Your soul joins theirs, if souls survive at all;
    You, gracious friend, are numbered with the blest.
Safe in the urn I pray your bones may rest,
    And earth weigh lightly in your burial.

Tristia 5.7 (with omissions)

I occupy my mind, beguile my sorrows,
    And do my best to cheat the cares that cark.
What better do, alone on this forsaken
    Coastline? What else to try for ills so bad?
If I look at the place, it's most unlovely
    And nothing in the world can be more sad,
Or at the men, they're not worth calling human;
    Wilder than wolves is their ferocity.
A few retain some trace of the Greek language,
    But that's made barbarous by the Getic twang.
There's not one single soul among these people
    Who might use Latin words, however basic;
And I, the bard of Rome – forgive me, Muses! –
    For most things am compelled to use Sarmasic.

Amores 3.9 (with omissions)

If for Achilles, if for Memnon dead,
    Their mothers grieved, if goddesses can mourn,
Weep, Elegy, and loose your hair forlorn –
    Too truly you are named from sad tears shed.
Tibullus, your own bard, your glory, now
    On the tall pyre, a futile corpse, is burned.
When evil fate dooms good men, may I be
    Forgiven if I've no faith in gods at all!
Live righteously – you die; in prayer take pains –
    Death drags you from the temple to the tomb.
Trust in good verse – Tibullus, look, lies dumb;
    A little urn can hold what now remains.
And yet, if aught survives but shade and name,
    Tibullus dwells in some Elysian glade;

Appendix 1: Notes on syntax

The following notes explain constructions that have not been taught in Parts I to III of the Oxford Latin Course. Wherever these occur in the text of the Reader, they are glossed without explanation. These notes enable teachers to explain the constructions, if they wish, and to answer questions students may ask.

References are given by the page and line numbers of the Reader.

Historic infinitive

Sometimes the present infinitive is used instead of the indicative in narrative (with the subject in the nominative) to describe exciting or striking actions or emotions; it is used commonly by the historians (hence its name), e.g.

Sabinus ... trepidare et concursare cohortisque disponere. (Caesar, p. 86, ll. 69–70)
Sabinus ... panicked and ran up and down and arranged his cohorts.

> **pars ducere muros**
> **molirique arcem et manibus subvolvere saxa,**
> **pars optare locum tecto et concludere sulco.**
> (Virgil, pp. 144–6, ll. 51–3)

Some were building walls and toiling at the citadel and rolling up stones with their hands, some were choosing a place for a building and enclosing it with a trench.

neque Hasdrubal alium quemquam praeficere malle ubi quid fortiter ac strenue agendum esset, neque milites alio duce plus confidere aut audere. (Livy, p. 170, ll. 27–9)
There was no one Hasdrubal preferred to put in command when there was need for any brave and strenuous action, nor did the soldiers show more confidence or daring under any other leader.

Supines

1 Supine in **-um**, e.g. **paratum**

This part of the verb has been learnt as the fourth principal part. It is the accusative case of a verbal noun and is used to express purpose after a verb expressing motion, e.g.

magna manu ad castra oppugnatum venerunt. (Caesar, p. 82, l. 6)
They came with a large force to the camp to attack it.

Sabinus ... interpretem suum ad eum mittit rogatum ... (Caesar, p. 86, ll. 95–6)
Sabinus ... sends his interpreter to him to ask ...

2 Supine in **-u**, e.g. **paratu**

This, a 4th declension ablative form, is used only as an ablative of respect after certain adjectives, e.g. **mirabile dictu** = 'wonderful to relate'. Compare:

principes Britanniae ... optimum factu esse duxerunt ... (Caesar, p. 64, ll. 119–22)
The princes of the Britons considered it best to do ...

quae quamquam foeda visu erant ... (Livy p. 178, l. 42)
Although this was dreadful to see ...

Comparative clauses

Comparative clauses are usually introduced by *correlatives* and have their verbs in the indicative. Such correlatives are:

sic ... ut	so ... as
idem ... qui	the same as
talis ... qualis	such as
tantus ... quantus	as great as
tot ... quot	as many as
totiens ... quotiens	as often as

eadem quae Ambiorix cum Sabino egerat commemorant. (Caesar, p. 92, ll. 36–7)
They list the same arguments as Ambiorix had used with Sabinus.

illud soleo admirari, non me totiens accipere tuas litteras, quotiens a Quinto mihi fratre adferantur. (Cicero, p. 32, ll. 128–9)
I'm often surprised at this, that I don't get letters from you as often as they are delivered from my brother Quintus.

The relative clause often comes first, e.g.

utque ego maiores, sic me coluere minores. (Ovid, p. 194, l. 45)
As I (worshipped) older (poets), so younger ones worshipped me.

qualis ... exercet Diana choros ... talis erat Dido. (Virgil, p. 146, ll. 71–6)
Like Diana (when she) starts the dances ... such was Dido.

quanto erat in dies gravior ... oppugnatio, tanto crebriores litterae nuntiique ad Caesarem mittebantur. (Caesar, p. 94, ll. 92–3)
The more serious the attack became day by day, the more frequent were the letters and messengers sent to Caesar (literally, 'by how much more serious ... by so much more frequent ...').

quo propius ea contentio ... accedit, eo clarius periculum apparet. (Caelius to Cicero, p. 42, ll. 59–60)
The nearer this struggle approaches, the clearer the danger is (literally, 'by what nearer ... by that clearer ...').

Sometimes the second of the correlatives is omitted, e.g.

quotque aderant vates, rebar adesse deos. (Ovid, p. 194, l. 38)
As many poets were present, I thought gods were present (i.e. I thought all the poets present were gods).

Uses of the relative with the subjunctive

1 The relative with the subjunctive is often used to express *purpose*, e.g.

equites a Q. Atrio ad Caesarem venerunt qui nuntiarent ... (Caesar, p. 74, l. 45)
Cavalry came from Q. Atrius to Caesar to announce ...

2 The relative with the subjunctive can express *cause*:

tum demum Sabinus, qui nihil ante providisset, trepidare et concursare. (Caesar, p. 86, ll. 69–70)
Then Sabinus, because he had foreseen nothing, began to panic and rush about.

peccasse mihi videor qui a te discesserim. (Cicero, p. 42, ll. 74–5)
I feel (I seem to myself) I have done wrong in leaving you (because I/who left you).

3 Consecutive relative, i.e. the relative clause expresses *consequence*, e.g.

dignus est qui puniatur.
He is worthy/deserves to be punished.

4 After a demonstrative (**is, ea, id** etc.), where the relative means 'of such a kind that ...', e.g.

neque is sum ... qui gravissime ex vobis mortis periculo terrear. (Caesar, p. 84, ll. 48–9)
Nor am I the sort of person to be terrified by danger of death most of all of you.

ea est Romana gens quae victa quiescere nesciat. (Livy 9.3.12)
The Roman race is such that it does not know how to rest after defeat.

quin and quominus

quin (= **qui**, an old ablative form + **ne**) = 'by which not', 'so that not'. It is used after verbs of hindering, preventing, forbidding etc., when they are negatived, e.g.

praeterire ... non potui quin ... scriberem ad te. (Cicero, p. 44, ll. 4–5)
I could not fail to write to you (literally, 'I could not omit so that I did not write to you').

quin is also used after verbs of doubting and denying when they are negatived, e.g.

illud non dubito quin ... respublica nos inter nos ... coniunctura sit. (Cicero, p. 22, ll. 11–13)
I have no doubt of this, that political interest will unite us together.

haud dubia res visa quin per invia ... circumduceret agmen. (Livy, p. 182, ll. 28–9)
There seemed no doubt that he would (have to) lead his column round through trackless areas (literally, 'The situation did not seem doubtful (but) that he should lead ...').

quominus (= 'by which the less', 'so that not') is used after verbs of hindering, preventing etc. whether negative or positive, e.g.

onerariae naves ... vento tenebantur quominus in eundem portum venire possent. (Caesar, p. 58, ll. 30–32)
The troop-carrying ships were held back by the wind so that they could not reach the same port/were prevented by the wind from reaching the same port.

Appendix 2: The Roman calendar

We have consistently glossed the many dates which occur in Cicero's letters, since we do not consider it necessary for students to master the cumbersome Roman calendar in detail, though they should perhaps have a general idea of how it worked. This appendix will enable teachers to explain to their students as much as they think necessary.

The twelve months of the Roman year were: *Ianuarius, Februarius, Martius, Aprilis, Maius, Iunius, Quintilis* (later *Iulius*), *Sextilis* (later *Augustus*), *September, October, November, December*. (The old Roman year started on 1 March, hence *Quintilis* = the fifth month, etc.).

Until Julius Caesar reformed the calendar in 46 BC, March, May, July and October each had thirty-one days, February had twenty-eight, the other months twenty-nine days each, giving a total of 355 days, ten days short of the true length of the solar year. At regular intervals an extra ('intercalary') month was inserted between February and March to correct the discrepancy.

Dates were calculated from three fixed points in the month: *Kalendae* = 1st; *Nonae* = 5th; *Idus* = 13th.

In March, May, July and October (i.e. the months which were thirty-one days long), however, the Nones came on the 7th and the Ides on the 15th of the month. Dates which fall on one of the fixed days are expressed in the ablative case, e.g. *Kalendis Aprilibus* = 1 April; *Idibus Martiis* = 15 March. Other dates are expressed in the accusative by counting backwards from the nearest fixed date, e.g. *pridie Kalendas Aprilis* = 31 March; *ante diem tertium Idus Martias* (the third day before the Ides of March) = 13 March (counting is inclusive, i.e. count Ides (15th), day before Ides, day before that); *ante diem quintum Nonas Maias* (the fifth day before the Nones of May) = 3 May (count Nones (7th) plus four days back).

Remember that the Kalends are not the last day of the month but the first day of the *next* month. For example, *ante diem sextum Kalendas Aprilis* (the sixth day before the Kalends of April) = 27 March (count the Kalends plus five days back).

Dates were usually abbreviated, e.g. *Kal. Mai.* (*Kalendis Mais*) = 1 May; *a.d. v Non. Mai.* (*ante diem quintum Nonas Maias*) = 3 May.

Cicero

Read the following passage carefully and then answer the questions below:

armatis hominibus ante diem tertium Nonas Novembris expulsi sunt fabri de
area nostra, Quinti fratris domus primo fracta coniectu lapidum ex area
nostra, deinde inflammata iussu Clodi inspectante urbe coniectis ignibus,
magna querela et gemitu hominum omnium. ille vel ante demens ruere, post
5 hunc vero furorem nihil nisi caedem inimicorum cogitare, vicatim ambire,
servis aperte spem libertatis ostendere.
　　　　itaque a.d. iii Id. Nov. cum Sacra via descenderem, insecutus est me
cum suis. clamor, lapides, fustes, gladii; et haec improvisa omnia. discessi in
vestibulum Tetti Damonis. qui erant mecum facile operas aditu prohibuerunt.
10 ipse occidi potuit; sed ego diaeta curare incipio, chirurgiae taedet.

1 Why was there building being done on **area nostra** (l. 2)?　　　　(2)

2 What did Clodius' gangs do to the workmen who were there?　　　　(2)

3 What two things happened to the house of Cicero's brother?　　　(2+2)

4 How did the people react to these outrages?　　　　(2)

5 What three things is Clodius up to now?　　　　(2+1+2)

6 Translate ll. 7–10 (**itaque ... potuit**).　　　　(15)

7 **clamor, lapides, fustes, gladii** (l. 8): this sentence has no verb.
　What is the effect of this?　　　　(3)

8 Explain what Cicero means by l. 10 (**sed ego ... taedet**).　　　　(3)

9 Under what circumstances do you think an episode of this kind
　could happen in a modern city?　　　　(4)

　　　　　　　　　　　　　　　　　　TOTAL:　　(40)

Caesar

(Teacher's note: this exercise must not be set until a reasonable amount of the Caesar selection has been read. If you wish to set it sooner, you must adapt question 7.)

Read the following passage carefully and then answer the questions below:

exigua parte aetatis reliqua Caesar, etsi in his locis maturae sunt hiemes, tamen in Britanniam proficisci contendit, quod omnibus fere Gallicis bellis hostibus nostris inde sumministrata auxilia intellegebat; et si tempus anni ad bellum gerendum deficeret, tamen magno sibi usui fore arbitrabatur, si
5 modo insulam adiisset et genus hominum perspexisset, loca, portus, aditus cognovisset; quae omnia fere Gallis erant incognita.

neque enim temere praeter mercatores illo adiit quisquam neque eis ipsis quicquam praeter oram maritimam atque eas regiones quae sunt contra Galliam notum est. itaque vocatis ad se undique mercatoribus, neque quanta
10 esset insulae magnitudo, neque quae aut quantae nationes incolerent, neque quem usum belli haberent aut quibus institutis uterentur, neque qui essent ad maiorem navium multitudinem idonei portus reperire poterat.

1 What two facts are we told in l. 1 which might lead us to believe
that Caesar's expedition to Britain was a rash undertaking?   (2+2)

2 What are we told in ll. 2–3 was the reason that Caesar decided to
go to Britain?   (3)

3 Translate ll. 3–6 (**et si tempus ... incognita**).   (15)

4 Who were the people who tended to go to Britain and what
regions did they get to know?   (2+1+2)

5 Who did Caesar summon? How useful did they prove as sources
of information?   (1+2)

6 What five things did he wish to discover from them?   (2+2+2+2+2)

7 How good do you feel Caesar's judgement to be? Do not
confine yourself to the passage printed above.   (5)

TOTAL: (45)

Catullus

Read the following poem carefully and then answer the questions below:

> multas per gentes et multa per aequora vectus
>   advenio has miseras, frater, ad inferias,
> ut te postremo donarem munere mortis
>   et mutam nequiquam alloquerer cinerem.
> 5 quandoquidem fortuna mihi tete abstulit ipsum,
>   heu miser indigne frater adempte mihi,
> nunc tamen interea haec, prisco quae more parentum
>   tradita sunt tristi munere ad inferias,
> accipe fraterno multum manantia fletu,
> 10   atque in perpetuum, frater, ave atque vale.

1 What are we told about the poet's journey and where he has
   come (ll. 1–2)?   (2+2)

2 What does the poet intend to do (ll. 3–4)? Explain why he sees
   what he plans to do as **nequiquam** (l. 4). Explain what the poet
   means by **cinerem** (l. 4).   (4+2+2)

3 What has fortune done to the poet (ll. 5–6)? What is the poet's
   reaction to this?   (2+1)

4 What is the poet planning to do (ll. 7–8)? Give two reasons
   why he is intending to do this.   (2+2+2)

5 Translate ll. 9–10 (**accipe ... vale**).   (8)

6 What do we call the verse form in which this poem is written?
   Write out and scan ll. 1–2 (**multas ... inferias**), showing the
   arrangement of heavy and light syllables and the division
   into feet.   (1+4)

7 What is the emotion conveyed by this poem? Discuss some of
   the ways in which this emotion is conveyed.   (6)

                                              TOTAL: (40)

Virgil

Read the following passage carefully and then answer the questions below:

> illa, gravis oculos conata attollere, rursus
> deficit; infixum stridit sub pectore vulnus.
> ter sese attollens cubitoque adnixa levavit,
> ter revoluta toro est oculisque errantibus alto
> quaesivit caelo lucem ingemuitque reperta.
>   tum Iuno omnipotens longum miserata dolorem
> difficilisque obitus Irim demisit Olympo
> quae luctantem animam nexosque resolveret artus.
> nam quia nec fato merita nec morte peribat,
> sed misera ante diem subitoque accensa furore,
> nondum illi flavum Proserpina vertice crinem
> abstulerat Stygioque caput damnaverat Orco.
> ergo Iris croceis per caelum roscida pennis
> mille trahens varios adverso sole colores
> devolat et supra caput astitit. 'hunc ego Diti
> sacrum iussa fero teque isto corpore solvo.'
> sic ait et dextra crinem secat: omnis et una
> dilapsus calor atque in ventos vita recessit.

Line numbers: 5, 10, 15

1 Describe the last moments of Dido (ll. 1–5). Comment on two ways in which the rhythm and sound of l. 2 (**deficit ... vulnus**) help to express the sense. (8+2+2)

2 Translate ll. 6–8 (**tum ... artus**). (8)

3 What had Proserpine not done (ll. 11–12)? Why (ll. 9–10)? (4+4)

4 Describe Iris as Virgil shows her (ll. 13–14). (4)

5 Who is Dis (l. 15)? (2)

6 What does Iris do to Dido (l. 17)? What is the result of this action? (2+2)

7 Write out and scan l. 17 (**sic ... una**), showing the arrangement of heavy and light syllables and the division into feet. (2)

8 'After the unbearable climax, the book ends in tranquillity.' Do you feel that this is the 'right' ending? Give reasons for your answer. (5)

TOTAL: (50)

Livy

(Teacher's note: this exercise must not be set until a reasonable amount of the Livy selection has been read. If you wish to set it sooner, you must adapt question 8.)

Read the following passage carefully and then answer the questions below it:

Hannibal, navium agmen, ad excipiendum adversi impetum fluminis, parte superiore transmittens tranquillitatem infra traicientibus lintribus praebebat. Galli occursant in ripa cum variis ululatibus cantuque moris sui, quatientes scuta super capita vibrantesque dextris tela, quamquam ex adverso terrebat
5 tanta vis navium cum ingenti sono fluminis et clamore vario nautarum militumque, et qui nitebantur perrumpere impetum fluminis et qui ex altera ripa traicientes suos hortabantur.
    iam satis paventes adverso tumultu terribilior ab tergo adortus clamor, castris ab Hannone captis. mox et ipse aderat ancepsque terror circumstabat,
10 et e navibus tanta vi armatorum in terram evadente et ab tergo improvisa premente acie. Galli postquam utroque vim facere conati pellebantur, qua patere visum maxime iter perrumpunt trepidique in vicos passim suos diffugiunt. Hannibal, ceteris copiis per otium traiectis, spernens iam Gallicos tumultus castra locat.

1 Which river is being crossed (l. 1)? (1)

2 What was the problem about the crossing referred to in l. 1?
   How did Hannibal solve it? (3+3)

3 Describe the actions of the Gauls in ll. 3–4 (**Galli ... tela**). (6)

4 Describe the ways in which Hannibal's fleet and his men had a
   terrifying effect on the Gauls (ll. 4–6). (6)

5 What added to their fear (l. 8)? Why did this arise? (2+2)

6 What exactly was the **anceps terror** (ll. 9–11)? (2+2)

7 Translate ll. 11–13 (**Galli ... diffugiunt**). (13)

8 How effective was Hannibal at overcoming difficulties? Give
   reasons for the points you make. Do not confine your answer
   to the passage printed above. (5)

TOTAL: (45)

Ovid

Read the following poem carefully and then answer the questions below it:

psittacus, Eois imitatrix ales ab Indis,
    occidit: exsequias ite frequenter, aves;
ite, piae volucres, et plangite pectora pinnis
    et rigido teneras ungue notate genas.
5 omnes, quae liquido libratis in aere cursus,
    tu tamen ante alios, turtur amice, dole.
plena fuit vobis omni concordia vita
    et stetit ad finem longa tenaxque fides.
quid tamen ista fides, quid rari forma coloris,
10   quid vox mutandis ingeniosa sonis,
quid iuvat, ut datus es, nostrae placuisse puellae?
    infelix avium gloria nempe iaces.
occidit illa loquax humanae vocis imago
    psittacus, extremo munus ab orbe datum.
15 septima lux venit non exhibitura sequentem;
    clamavit moriens lingua 'Corinna, vale.'

1 Where did the parrot come from? Who do you suppose gave
   it to Corinna? What has happened to it?   (2+1+1)

2 Translate **piae** (l. 3). How does the sound of this line help to
   express the sense?   (1+2)

3 In l. 4, what is the effect the poet achieves by putting the words
   rigido and **teneras** next to each other?   (2)

4 Why is the turtle dove asked to grieve especially (ll. 6–8)?   (2)

5 **quid ... quid ... quid ... quid ...** (ll. 9–11): what is the answer to
   these questions (one English word)? What facts about the bird
   does the poet list here, and which do you think he intends to be
   the most important?   (1+4+1)

6 Translate ll. 12–14 (**infelix ... datum**).   (10)

7 What two things are we told about the parrot's death in ll. 15–16?   (2+2)

8 Ovid writes this lament for Corinna's parrot as though the bird
   was a human being. Find and describe two examples in the poem
   of the parrot or other birds being described in human terms.   (2+2)

                                        TOTAL: (35)

Answers to the exercises

Cicero

1 Clodius' gangs had destroyed Cicero's house (2).
2 They drove them out (2).
3 It was smashed up by pelted stones (2) and then set on fire (2).
4 They complained (1) and groaned (1).
5 He is planning to slaughter his enemies (2), going round the streets (1) and openly offering hope of freedom to slaves (2).
6 And so on 11 November when I was going down the Sacred Way, he chased me with his men. (There was) shouting, stones, clubs, swords (were wielded); and all of this was unforeseen. I left the road (and fled) into the forecourt of Tettius Damo's house. Those who were with me easily stopped his gangs from approaching. (Clodius) could have been killed (15).
7 The complete chaos and speed of the action are reflected (3).
8 Cicero is tired of all the violence (surgery); he feels that a gentler, more lasting approach (a diet) is called for (3).
9 Impressionistic marking for this answer (4).

Caesar

1 There was not much summer left (2) and winters come early in this region (2).
2 In almost all the Gallic wars help had been provided for our enemies from there (3).
3 And if the time of year was far from ideal (literally, failed) for waging war, he still/even so thought it would be of great use to him if only he had come to the island and seen the kind of men (that lived there, (and) found out about the localities, harbours and approaches); all of these things were almost unknown to the Gauls (10).
4 The merchants (2), who got to know the sea shore (1) and those regions which face Gaul (2).
5 The merchants (1), who proved useless (2).
6 He wished to discover: how large the island was (2); which nations lived there and how big they were (2); what was their method of warfare (2); what their way of life was (2); and what harbours were suitable for a large number of (fairly) big ships (2).
7 Impressionistic marking for this answer (5).

Catullus

1 He has travelled through many nations (1) and over many seas (1) to visit his brother's tomb ('to Troy' is a satisfactory answer) (2).
2 He intends to make an offering to his dead brother (2) and to speak to his ashes (2). The action of l. 4 will be **nequiquam** because the ashes will not be able to reply (2; 1 mark can be given if the student says that the ashes are deaf). The corpse has been cremated (2).
3 It has taken his brother away from him (2). He is distressed/angry/indignant about this (1).
4 He is planning to give offerings to his brother (2). It is the ancient custom (of their forefathers) (2); and it is his (sad) duty (2).
5 Receive them (these gifts), all wet with a/your brother's tears, and for ever, brother, hail and farewell (8).
6 Elegiac couplets (1).

    mūltās | pēr gēn|tēs ∧ ēt | mūltă pěr | āēquŏră | vēctŭs

    ādvěnǐ(o) | hās mǐsěr|ās, ∧ frātěr, ăd| īnfěrǐ|ās (4).

7 Impressionistic marking for this answer (6).

Virgil

1 She tried to raise her eyes but failed (2). She raised herself three times on her elbow (3) but each time she fell back (1). She looked for the light in the sky (1) and groaned when she found it (1). The enjambement (this word does not have to be used but its meaning must come across) at the start of the line reflects her failure to lift her eyes (2). The **s** sounds reflect the hissing of the wound (2; 1 mark can be given if the student refers only to the 'hard' **d**, **p** and **t**s).
2 Then all-powerful Juno, pitying her long pain and (her) difficult death, sent down Iris from Olympus to free her struggling spirit and (loose) her close-locked limbs (8).
3 She had not yet taken a (golden) lock from her hair (2) and thus condemned her (life) to Orcus (the underworld) (2). Dido was dying neither through fate (1) nor in a death she had deserved (1) but before her time (1) and suddenly (in a sudden frenzy) (1).
4 With dew on her saffron wings (2) and drawing (behind her) a thousand different colours as the sun shone on her (2).
5 Dis is the god/king of the underworld (2).
6 She cuts off (a lock of) her hair (2); Dido now dies (all heat slipped from her and her life went away into the winds) (2).

7   sīc ăĭt | ēt dēx | trā ∧ crīn|ēm sěcăt: | ōmnĭs ět | ūnā (2).

8 Impressionistic marking for this answer (5).

Livy

1 The Rhône (1).
2 The current (2) might wash them away (1). He sent the (column of) ships across upstream (3).
3 They rush to meet them on the bank (2) with various war-whoops and with singing (2), shaking their shields and brandishing their spears (2).
4 There were so great a number/fleet of ships (so many strong ships) (2), a huge noise from the river (2) and shouting from the sailors and soldiers (2).
5 A more terrible shout from behind (2); Hanno had taken their camp (2).
6 So many armed man landing (on the bank) (2) and troops unexpectedly harrying them from the rear (2).
7 After the Gauls, having tried to fight in both directions, were (being) driven back, they broke through by the route which seemed to offer the best escape and fled in panic in different directions to their villages (13).
8 Impressionistic marking for this answer (5).

Ovid

1 The parrot came from the East Indies (2). The poet/Ovid gave it to Corinna (1). It has died (1).
2 Good/virtuous/dutiful/pious (1). The alliteration of **p**s (1) reflects the beating of the wings (1).
3 He emphasizes the harshness of their claws against the softness of their cheeks (2).
4 They had lived in harmony all their lives (1) and been faithful to the end (1).
5 Nothing (1). The qualities: fidelity/faithfulness (1), unusual colour (1), adaptable voice (1), a pleasing present for the girl (1). The last (1).
6 Wretched glory of birds, (to be sure/certainly) you lie (dead). That garrulous echo of the human voice has died, the parrot, a present given from the edge of the world (10).
7 It died on the seventh day (2). Its dying words were 'Corinna, farewell/goodbye' (2).
8 Impressionistic marking for this answer. The two most obvious examples are in ll. 3–4 when the birds are invited to behave like human mourners, beating their breasts and tearing their cheeks (2+2).